CREATING
TOPIARY

GERALDINE LACEY

GARDEN · ART · PRESS

© 1987 Geraldine Lacey
World copyright reserved
First published 1987
Reprinted 1988, 1992

ISBN 1 870673 00 X

British Library CIP Data
Lacey, Geraldine
    Creating topiary
    1. Topiary work
    I. Title
    715.1   SB463

ISBN 187067300X

Endpapers:
Front: Penshurst Place, Kent.
Back: Ladew, Maryland, U.S.A.
Frontispiece: A garden in Hampshire with topiary birds and hedging.

Published by Garden Art Press,
a division of Antique Collectors' Club Ltd.
Printed in England by the Antique Collectors' Club Ltd., Woodbridge, Suffolk

For my mother

Colour Plates

Contents

Introduction

Topiary may be an ancient art but it is also a very personal one. There is something about the shaping of plants and hedges that brings out an excitement and pleasure that is distinctly individual. In the years I have spent preparing this book, travelling in Europe and America, I have had the good fortune to visit gardens great and small, to see classic, famous specimens, and to stumble upon wonderful whimsy hidden to all but the sharpest-eyed pedestrian. In every case the anticipation and fulfilment have been sharpened by the delight I have obtained from the topiary involved. Sometimes the investigation and the chase have led to disappointment, when the yew trees have outgrown themselves or the cultivator has died and his work been obliterated. On certain occasions I have entered once-famous gardens to find them sadly untended, the house empty and the hedges, once battlemented, now turning into wild boundaries. Mostly, however, my excited anticipation has been rewarded and the results are illustrated in this book.

In preparing a publication on topiary I have been very much aware that there is no specialist volume currently in print and that this wonderful subject has been neglected by publishers since the work of Miles Hadfield and Nathaniel Lloyd superseded that of Curtis and Gibson. Jekyll and Hussey's work, *Garden Ornament*, has a meritorious section on topiary, but the excellent photographs illustrate gardens which the modern owner might find very costly to maintain. Furthermore, there is little indication of how the specimens were created.

Today's interest in topiary is perhaps less historical and more concerned with the creation of new specimens, so that certain garden books have brief sections on this, but they are not specialist works. For this reason, I have reluctantly confined the fascinating historical aspects of topiary to an initial chapter although, naturally, the history of some of the celebrated gardens illustrated later in the book is briefly outlined. I have deliberately set out, in the middle chapters, to show how foundations of a topiary garden can be laid and how individual specimens can be created, since previous books have not provided any detailed exposition of this. There is now much interest in topiary and many would-be enthusiasts looking for advice will, I hope, be assisted by these chapters. Subsequently, the book deals with well-established gardens and amusing as well as formal specimens.

In moving with the times I have introduced what may be considered a controversial element into this book. This concerns the use of wire frames for shaping and the production of pre-formed topiary using moss-filled structures. Traditional topiarists tend to frown upon these modern systems, although the use of wire frames dates back a considerable time and is really just an aid to the production of traditional forms. Pre-formed 'topiary' is arguably not the same thing at all; it does not try to give an impression of springing naturally from its surroundings. Pre-formed 'topiary' makes no excuse for being purely a decorative fancy, not necessarily appropriate to a garden and often used, as at Chelsea and in America, as a spectacular feature of tourist attraction. Since this book is about topiary in all its aspects and covers such items as ornamental town plants in tubs I felt that, to be complete, it should take in the amazingly professional pre-formed topiary of the moss-filled frame. At Longwood Gardens in Pennsylvania both traditional and pre-formed topiary provide two of the multiple attractions of a widely-based and justifiably celebrated garden.

The search for suitable specimens has led me to form many rewarding friendships and to discover extraordinary creations. When I first started recording the details of Brickwall's chess garden, I thought that it would be unique. I was soon led to Hever Castle, where the golden yew chess pieces are highly developed. Later I found myself at Little Haseley, where the magnificent chess garden provided some of the best illustrations. As though this were not enough, a kindly tip from the photographer Michael Boys led me to a charming chess garden in the grounds of an ancient house belonging to a famous lady author. It has therefore been a voyage of discovery to produce this book, not only in terms of finding the specimens involved but also in the personal idiosyncracies of maintenance and production by the individual owners. Not everyone clips their specimens at the same time of year, or in the same way, or with the same instruments. My summary of the most widely-used methods is therefore made with the humble reservation that the information is not absolute and that differences of opinion exist between gardeners.

During the preparation of the book it seems to have rained ceaselessly, not only in England but also — heavily — in Holland, persistently in Italy, and unkindly in America at a time when it shouldn't have. A gift of a box peacock from a generous Dutch grower was impounded temporarily by British Customs, who thought it was a tree; an Italian gardener at Torrigiani thought that the elephant at Garzoni which I described in pidgin Italian was a real one and expressed astonishment at the lengths to which rival Garzoni was going to attract tourists; the architect at Bristol explained that he created his full-size privet locomotive because the hedge from which it was created took too long to cut! Many impressions stay in my mind. A long journey to Ledbury in Herefordshire to record the famous cottage topiary of a horse and jockey ended sadly when it transpired that hard winters had destroyed Mr. Flower's loving creations but, in visiting the nearby churchyard, I did find his remaining work in the guardian angel of yew standing at the head of a grave under a nearby tree, full size and sculptural, its hands at prayer. Throughout my travels everyone concerned with topiary has been incredibly and generously helpful, so that it is invidious to single out one individual, but Mrs. Pat Hammer of Longwood must be mentioned for her enthusiasm and unstinting help. If, lastly, I could choose any one individual specimen to take home with me for my permanent delight, it would in fact be a pair — the astounding birds of Sapperton, Gloucestershire, which stand in a cottage garden, on their layer-sliced columns, soaring up high to perch above the surrounding roofs in an extraordinary burst of artistry in yew.

Since starting this book I have been struck by the transient nature of some of the specimens and have determined to try and keep a record of as many as possible that are in existence. Any information or photographic contributions that would assist in this record would be greatly appreciated.

Hartwell House topiary painted by Balthazar Nebot in 1738.

Hartwell House gardens painted by Nebot in 1738, showing part of the house, with gardeners sharpening scythes.

Chapter One
HISTORICAL BACKGROUND

Like much of European civilisation, topiary can be traced back to the Greeks, with their love of the orders and of formality. From Greece it inevitably came to Rome — classical topiary was the perfect foil to the Roman villa. The cool influence of trees could be brought right up to the house with no loss of order or architectural impact. The Roman Empire spread the practice of disposing trees in formal patterns like the quincunx (five trees arranged so that one is at each corner of a square or box and one is in the centre) and of using topiary to regulate the planning of the garden. Examples were to be found all over Europe, including Britain. With the passing of the Roman Empire, however, the Dark Ages destroyed much of this aspect of gardening and in England topiary was completely forgotten until the Norman Conquest, when the Roman art which had been well established in France returned to the British Isles.

By the twelfth century romantic mazes and labyrinths of clipped evergreens had become the fashion and the trail is picked up again, especially at the park of Woodstock in 1123 where Henry I enjoyed the labyrinth containing a bower associated ultimately with Fair Rosamund Clifford, the great love of Henry II's life.

In the thirteenth century the rage for formal gardening had particularly affected Holland where, because every square foot of land was precious, gardens were laid out with mathematical precision and the consequent primness was carried over into the trees and plants themselves. The visitor to modern Holland can, of course, still see this in the contemporary Dutch garden, and it is interesting that the Dutch still retain a tradition of box topiary — concentrated in the Boskoop area — which is described in detail in Chapter 8 of this book.

What has been described as the Golden Age of topiary, however, did not start in Britain until the sixteenth century, when it coincided understandably with the growth of wealth and commerce associated with the Renaissance. Gardening became more and more popular. To the existing indigenous styles were added the sophistication of the French and the Dutch schools. A steady progression of evidence refers the researcher to Wrexhill Castle at Howden in Yorkshire (Leland, 1540), where there were 'mounts, opere topiorii, writhen about with degrees like the turnings in cockil shelles', which were presumably the formal spirals of yesteryear, and to Canons Ashby, Northamptonshire, with its clipped yews of 1550 onwards. From there the trail lead on to many other examples all over the country, culminating perhaps in Beaumont's work at Levens Hall and Hampton Court, although it should be mentioned that Beaumont worked as far afield as Ashton Park and Stoneyhurst in Lancashire to Forde Abbey in Dorset.

The trail to Levens starts perhaps at Versailles, where the great French garden planner, Le Nôtre, laid out the scheme. Beaumont, a disciple of Le Nôtre's, laid out the semicircular garden at Hampton Court, and eventually became gardener to James II. Alas, Hampton Court has changed considerably since Beaumont's day, but at Levens Hall in Westmorland (now Cumbria), not far from Kendal, a magnificent legacy of that early work of Beaumont has been left for posterity to enjoy. As the plan below shows, the garden is based on a series of formal layouts which provided the framework for the topiary envisaged. The shapes at Levens, opposite, have since developed into a series of forms and sculpturally abstract entities which are quite unique, even though some of them have provided the model for many imitators. Levens is a remarkable heritage for

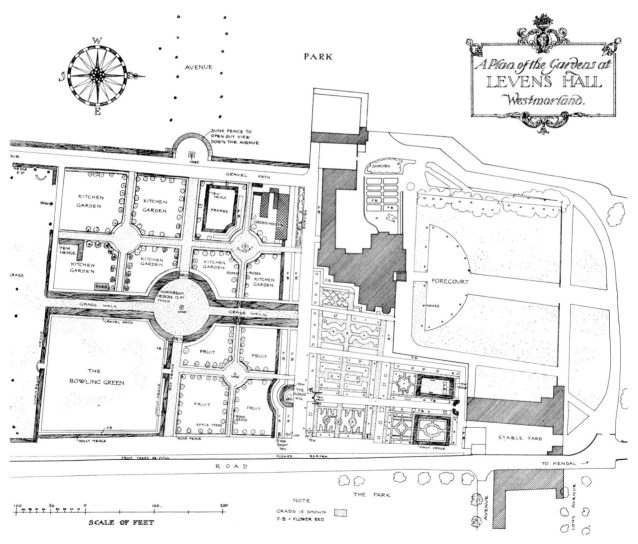

Plan of Levens Hall, laid out by Beaumont in 1690.

Levens Hall at the end of the 19th century, showing men at work clipping the specimens.

Levens — a general view of c.1900.

Levens Hall — the arch in about 1920.

THE OLD GARDENS AT BRICKWALL NEAR NORTHIAM : SUSSEX

*A view from the upper windows of Brickwall House, Northiam, Sussex, taken from
Blomfield's* The Formal Garden in England, *showing much of the original layout.*

the modern topiary enthusiast to admire and has been meticulously maintained,
so that the public can enjoy and appreciate the extent to which yews and other
trees can be modelled to the sculptural gardener's whim.

Not all topiary gardens were as grand as Hampton Court and Levens Hall, nor
did they need a Le Nôtre or a Beaumont to lay them out. Topiary gardening
reached its height in England when William and Mary were on the throne,
1689-1702, perhaps because William of Orange brought with him from Holland
a taste for clipped yews. More modest gardens than the royal ones and those
financed by the Keeper of the Privy Purse (at Levens) were attempted by gentry
keeping up with fashion. The illustration above shows the layout of Brickwall, the
manor house at Northiam, Sussex, where in 1680 Jane Frewen decided to lay out
a garden following her family's acquisition of the hundred year old house in 1666.
The lawn in front of the house was enclosed by high hedges and walls whilst the
geometric plan included parterres, arches and arbours. Again, this desire to
subdue nature provided for axial gravelled walks and, in accordance with the
'Dutch' taste, some topiary consisting of clipped yews in geometric shapes.

An interesting feature of Brickwall is that it is now being restored as a modern
topiary garden with a chess theme. The design for this garden, its layout and the
frames needed for the control of the shapes of the chessmen are the subject of
detailed examination in Chapter 6.

Every action provokes a reaction and never was this more true than in questions

Hartwell House gardens painted by Nebot in 1738, showing the allées and arcades, with gardeners working.

of taste. Inevitably, the eighteenth century saw the start of a strong return to 'nature', especially in view of the over-adornment and fantasy of the topiary work which abounded at that time. The illustrations here and on page 10, show the yew exhedra at Hartwell House, Buckinghamshire, painted by Balthazar Nebot in 1738. Since the yews must be about forty years old, this remarkable garden dated from the Golden Age and represents a style, theatrical in character, in which, for part of the garden, yews were cut into vistas resembling shutters on a stage.

As shapes became more complex and sophisticated, there was bound to be a section of informed taste which rebelled. The proliferation of weird shapes, animals, statuary, birds and other fancies led to an eighteenth century crusade against topiary, spearheaded in particular by Addison and Pope, who both wielded their pens in ferocious attacks on the forceful control of nature in the garden.

The transformation of the over-ornate, perhaps monotonous English gardens, to which the writers addressed

Hartwell House — the bowling green and octagon pond.

The circular garden at Chastleton Manor House, Oxfordshire, in the early 1900s. Individual box specimens are contained within a formal, circular yew hedge which was not in the original plan.

Chastleton Manor House — the circular garden as it is today.

their satire, was very rapid. Bridgeman and Kent, landscape gardeners who swept away trees and hedges, were followed by 'Capability' Brown, so that in the course of the fifty years between 1740 and 1790 the gardens of England, with a very few exceptions, were radically changed. Topiary ceased to be regarded as an element in garden design and only a limited number of survivors from the Golden Age have remained for us to enjoy.

Towards the end of the nineteenth century there appears to have been something of a revival in the art of topiary. The photographs of Chastleton Manor House and Balcarres show sophisticated gardens as they were in about 1900, although Chastleton dates back to 1700 and is a rare example of an entirely box topiary garden. They needed considerable labour to maintain. These gardens would have been in full splendour at about the time that Curtis and Gibson wrote *The Book of Topiary* in 1904, when Gibson was the gardener in charge of Levens Hall. The book claimed that, starting twenty years earlier, a strong revival in the art of topiary had taken place. Certainly the availability of much cheap labour and the wealth at the disposition of the grand country house owners must have encouraged many of them to indulge in as much formal control of trees and shrubs in fanciful shaping to their immediate whims. There were, as well, nurseries which specialised in the supply of ready-made topiary at Highgate, Kew and Crawley, taking the Dutch nurserymen of the Boskoop area as their model. Indeed, supplies were obtained from this area in addition to local growth and Holland was scoured for mature examples, which were uprooted with due care and shipped to England. A welter of birds, spirals, spires, balls, dogs, ships, pyramids and other shapes

A view of Balcarres, Fife, from the terrace, with parterre in the foreground.

such as jugs and beakers, not to mention teddy bears, are to be seen in old photographs of these nurserymen's premises. Although the English ones have not survived, the reader can get an idea of what these nurseries were like from the photographs in Chapter 8, which illustrate surviving specialised nurseries in Holland today.

Individual gardens continued to provide examples of new topiary work into the twentieth century, but it seems that by 1950 topiary had once again declined. The reasons for this are probably a combination of many factors, not the least fashion — yet again, but questions of cost and time were also likely to be paramount. Dutch nurserymen were brought over to England to cultivate topiary until the Second World War and, in some particular cases, still carry on the maintenance of remarkable gardens. On the whole, however, topiary was regarded as idiosyncratic or, at least, an amusing survival of a previous eccentricity.

The tremendous revival in gardening and of interest in the theory and history of gardening which has taken place in the last ten years or so has brought renewed interest in topiary. Rather than using topiary for merely fanciful purposes, the modern gardener sees the formal arrangement of trees and shrubs as, firstly, providing essential structure to the garden. Shaping can be used to give sculptural emphasis where it is needed and, subsequently, the delight of the individual gardener in making a form which pleases his or her eye, be that form animal, abstract or ornamental, has once again become popular. This happy return to fashion comes at a time when the pleasure of gardening has reached an intensity which shows no sign of abating.

Chapter Two
HOW TO START
A TOPIARY GARDEN

Site

For many people the idea of topiary comes when an individual bush or small tree in the garden suggests a particular shape to them. This shape may be animal or abstract in a symmetrical form. It may just be a ball, a cone, or a spiral. Such creations of time and place provide a delightful individual specimen and many examples of these are given in this book, but topiary, throughout its history, has had an important function to perform in terms of the formal planning of a garden. Its origins come from the control of the environment round a building in Mediterranean circumstances and its development follows that of European civilisation.

Nowadays the sheer mobility of modern life and working careers tends to discourage a long-term view of a garden. This perhaps also tends to discourage younger gardeners from the idea of topiary in the sense of starting from scratch, but it is possible to create a mature-looking garden much faster than is often supposed. Although a period of ten years may, at the point of initiation, seem a long time, it is worth remembering that the plants, particularly the evergreens, are attractive whilst growing and that enjoyment is not only obtained by contemplating the mature result.

The choice of site for a topiary garden is vitally important. Sunlight is essential to produce dense and vigorous growth of an even nature. It is fairly obvious that if some of the plants are in shaded areas their growth will be uneven and they will not keep up with those in full sunlight. Even hardy performers like yew and box will produce ragged, random growth if placed in dark corners and, when shaping is required, imperfections will be glaringly exposed. Many topiary specialists prefer an area that is slightly below the level of the surrounding garden since they like to look at the specimens from an angle which is slightly above them. This requirement for a sunken garden is not, however, very easy for many gardens to fulfil in practice, and the nearest substitute recommended is to create a raised terrace to the north side of the topiary garden which will not interfere with the sunlight. All these requirements are basically connected with the need for shelter, since carefully-clipped specimens, even the heavy and dense yew, will suffer badly if beset by strong winds which damage and distort the branches.

The easiest way to provide shelter for the topiary is to plant hedges, if these do not already exist. Hedges provide excellent formal boundaries to the garden and

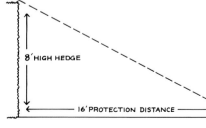

8′ HIGH HEDGE

16′ PROTECTION DISTANCE

A hedge protects for a distance twice its height on the leeward side.

Athelhampton, Dorset, showing the raised terrace from which the garden can be viewed.

Pienza in Italy — a simple, yet bold layout for this garden.

19

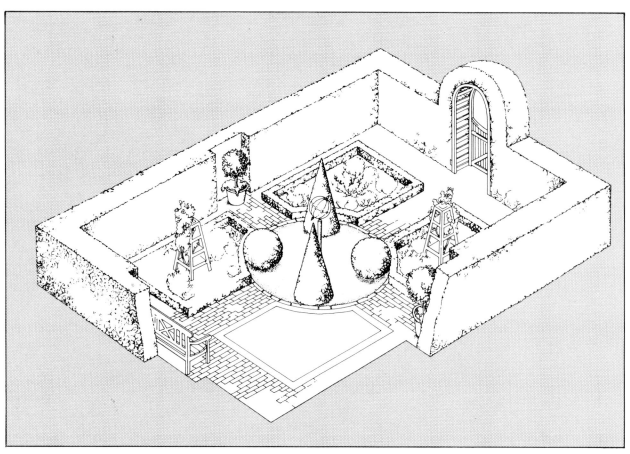

A simple rectangular garden enclosed by a hedge. The internal layout can be made simpler or more elaborate as required. Ideas for different hedge and specimen designs are illustrated throughout this book, while Chapter 6 includes a plan with dimensions which could be adapted for this garden.

can be used to divide it into 'rooms' with individual ornamental interest. The most common plants for hedges are yew, box, holly, beech, hornbeam and various conifers of the cypress derivation such as leylandii and thuyas. In Chapter 3 a detailed list of hedges and the general principles involved in planting and maintaining them is set out. Not only do such hedges have a functional sheltering purpose; they can be clipped to provide part of the topiary itself.

The height of the hedge in relation to its ability to give wind shelter is fixed by simple two-to-one calculation, i.e. the hedge protects for a distance of twice its height on the leeward side.

Garden plan

Clearly the planning of the site will depend on the space available and this will dictate the number of trees or bushes to be planted and the layout involved. In general, however, as a principle, the initial design should be kept as simple as possible. The proposed area should be mapped out into squares, not all of them necessarily the same size, but with a uniform coherence that will assist the identifiable axes of the garden, walks and paths that it is to contain. In the past, such gardens nearly always had large areas of flower beds, formally bordered, to set off the topiary, but nowadays it is quite usual to plant on grass to save labour. When the area and the plan have been broadly defined, another major consideration is the number of trees and the time required for clipping and maintenance. Trees should not be planted too closely together because they will

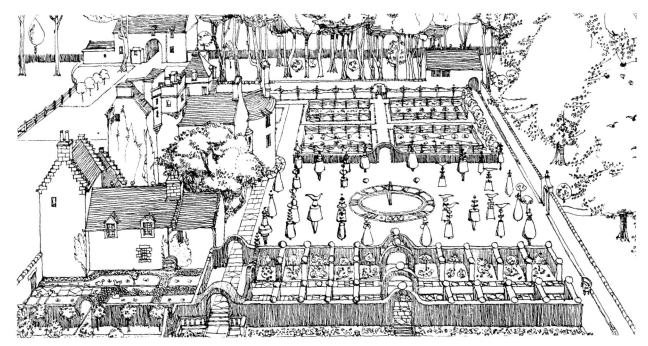

An elaborate garden plan at Earlshall, Fife, using hedging and specimen topiary.

grow strongly and densely, creating an entirely different environment than that which is seen at the bare beginnings. If they create overcrowding later they will suffer and the aspect will not be satisfactory.

Soil

As a general rule it is best to acquire plants from a nursery with similar soil and conditions to your own. If the soil, wind and site of a nearby nursery are comparable you are very fortunate, but these ideal conditions are difficult to meet. Most of the plants recommended for topiary work are fairly tolerant of soil types, but there are certain varieties with special requirements and these are listed in the characteristics in the next two chapters. A great deal of the secret of success lies in the preparation of the soil once the site plan has been determined. Topiary gardens are longer-term projects than usual plantings and it is worth building the structure on a careful and solid foundation. For this reason it makes sense to be quite clear about the preparation involved before you actually make a start.

Once the site and the plan of the garden have been decided, the practical enjoyment of planting the hedges and the specimens can begin. The principles involved and practical details of this work are described in the following chapters.

Check List — Site

Sunlight — must have full sunlight for vigorous growth
Screening — shelter from wind essential
Area — level
Space — as large as possible
Accessibility — reduces work
View — for maximum pleasure

Check List — Plan

Keep it simple
Divide into squares
Think of time required for maintenance
Consider different viewing angles
Allow space in front and behind for maintenance
Plant trees well apart
Avoid overcrowding

Formal hedge at Godington Park, Kent, showing both an architectural echo of the gables of the house and the 'pillar-box' feature of the corners of the hedge.

Ladew, Maryland, U.S.A., showing the 'windows' which allow distant views across the countryside. The dramatic silhouette of the top of the hedge involves pointed finials linked by handsome swags.

Gamberaia, Tuscany, Italy, showing the use of arched arcading in a hedge. The formal colonnade around the pool is enhanced by dwarf hedging which follows the curve.

22

Chapter Three
HEDGES

Hedges provide the most striking physical evidence of a garden. They tell the visitor something about the garden's owner. Hedges are required not only for shelter and the definition of the boundaries of a garden, they are the essential girders supporting the structure. It is therefore right that they should command serious thought and that time should be given to their design, their type and their form.

Hedges are used to provide the proportion and the architectural configuration of a garden. Although it is possible to use walls and fences to do this as well, it is worth bearing in mind that hedges cost less than fences and walls. They are often a much more harmonious way of defining the garden structure and of dividing the area into the separate, hidden spaces which are revealed when the visitor is subtly guided down the paths which form part of the structural plan. There is no reason why hedges should not be quite simple, straightforward shapes of a rectangular or square section, although a vertical taper, known as a batter, improves reception of sunlight and rainfall by following the plant's natural progression. Hedges can also be rounded, curved or shaped depending on the correlation and harmony these variants bring to the rest of the garden.

Height is the most serious consideration when planning a hedge, for the height and the thickness of hedging set the proportion of the garden. If the hedge is too high the garden will look small and confined. If the hedge is too low the element of control and definition will be lost, quite apart from the shelter which a hedge is required to provide. Since it follows that the height, once decided, is a dimension which must be retained and which has to have a relationship with the thickness of the hedge, it is clear that the hedge must be of a variety which can be clipped and controlled with relative ease. Plants which grow rapidly or lose their uniformity and coherence are not likely to attract the topiary gardener, who is seeking formality and order as a background or possibly even as a feature. One of the pleasant possibilities of the topiary hedge is that its shape can echo architectural features of the house or buildings nearby, or it can be used to frame or offset a particular garden decoration. Another possibility lies in the formal shaping of the ends or corners of hedges to provide architectural features in themselves, making pillars or boxes at such points which, when combined with surmounting finials, enhance the structural role of the hedges.

An extension of the 'masonry' concept of hedging is the provision of 'windows' in the hedge which may take the form of open arches, portholes or rectangular window shapes, all of which give variation in the solid structure and allow distant views to delight the eye. In some cases, as at Sissinghurst Castle in Kent, the opening is designed to allow a tantalising glimpse of a further part of the garden which has different characteristics, thus providing a visual variation.

These large hedges define the boundaries or 'rooms' of a garden, but within them, low or 'dwarf' hedges can be used to provide a simple or intricate pattern which enhances specimen topiary. Low hedges are also used for formal framing of flower beds which add colour and interest to the garden.

Buxus sempervirens suffruticosa — a dwarf variety of box planted as a border hedge.

Beech hedge of thick, square section.

Types of hedge suitable for topiary gardens

BEECH (*Fagus sylvatica*)

Beech and hornbeam are the most popular deciduous hedge plants apart from privet and are considerably tougher. Beech has been used for very large topiary hedge work such as that shown at Levens. There is a similar very large beech arch at St. Nicholas, Richmond, Yorkshire, which requires ladders of fire brigade dimensions to reach its pinnacle for clipping.

Beech is hardy and tolerant of lime soils but likes good drainage. Its leaves turn russet and are retained throughout winter on young wood until the fresh green leaves of spring push off the old remainders. Copper beech (*Fagus sylvatica cuprea*) and purple beech (*Fagus sylvatica purpurea*), which is pale red in spring, darkening as the season progresses, can both be used for hedging and are very attractive. Deciduous hedges such as beech will withstand the smoky, polluted atmosphere of towns better than the evergreens, apart from holly.

Small box plants — the dwarf suffruticosa variety.

Box hedge (Buxus sempervirens).

BOX (*Buxus sempervirens*)

Common box is used, like yew, for both hedges and individual topiary specimens, but it does not grow as high as yew. There are many varieties of box, all evergreens, and there are variegated and coloured types in addition to the normal

Leylandii hedge approximately 12 feet high.

Arch created in leylandii hedge.

dark-to-middle green of *Buxus sempervirens.* Box makes excellent small hedges and is tolerant of much clipping provided that no frost is in evidence. It is very popular in the United States, especially in the South, and has been intensely studied and documented in that area.

A particularly frequent use for box is that of edging for flower beds, where the contrast of its controlled green colour is highly effective against the colours of the flowers. A variety of *Buxus sempervirens* known as *suffruticosa,* a dwarf species, is much used for this purpose. It can be kept to a height of a few inches by clipping, but if left unchecked will go on up to 3 feet high.

Box does not grow very quickly — it is slower than yew — and is mainly confined to garden heights of 4 feet or below. It grows a dense mat of roots that are retained fairly near the surface so that feeding by the application of manure on the surface areas around the plants is very effective. Like yew it does not like a sooty atmosphere.

End section of leylandii hedge illustrating sloping side or batter.

Conifers

LAWSON CYPRESS (*Chamaecyparis lawsoniana*)
Sparse when planted in an exposed site, but in a sheltered position makes fine hedges.

LEYLAND CYPRESS (*Cupressocyparis leylandii*)
Leylandii has now become a very well-known hedge variety which appears to be insensitive to conditions and which grows so vigorously that it is almost a disadvantage. It will reach tree height very rapidly but, if clipped, can be used to provide a clean-cut disciplined hedge without difficulty. It does, however, need clipping two or three times per season. It will also stand extreme seaside conditions.

MONTEREY CYPRESS (*Cupressus macrocarpa*)
This cypress likes milder weather, being susceptible to frost, but does well in seaside conditions. It stands clipping well and is a rapid grower.

Macrocarpa hedge.

25

Two different types of thuja hedge.

THUJA (*Thuja plicata*)

The thuja, or western red cedar, is a relative newcomer to formal hedging but has the attraction of being a rapid-growing and hardy conifer. It stands clipping well and is resistant to wind whilst providing a dense green hedge similar to yew but not quite as dark in colour. In America thuja is also used for topiary work.

Details of hawthorn hedging.

HAWTHORN (*Crataegus monogyna*)

Hawthorn provides an excellent impenetrable deciduous hedge which can be clipped with impunity. It can be used for topiary work as well as hedging. Its prevalence in agriculture as an all-purpose barrier between fields and along roads testifies to its hardy, tough character which is not much affected by the type of soil in which it finds itself.

HOLLY (*Ilex aquifolium*)

Holly is a glossy dark evergreen which can be used for both hedges and topiary. Variegated and gold varieties also exist. Unlike yew and box it will stand town atmospheres containing soot without complaint. It is also extremely strong, withstanding gale conditions whilst providing an impenetrable screen. Holly can be clipped hard and, although slow-growing, will continue into a large tree if not controlled, reaching a height of up to 20-25 feet when fully developed.

Holly grown as a hedge.

The hornbeam hedge and arch at Wisley in winter.

HORNBEAM (*Carpinus betulus*)

Common hornbeam is also very hardy and comparable with the beech in making a strong deciduous hedge with tight growth. Clipping in late summer helps the plant to retain its leaves throughout the winter.

Lonicera hedge.

LONICERA (*Lonicera nitida*)

The evergreen lonicera of this variety, known as the Chinese honeysuckle, makes a dense, dark green hedge which grows well in moist conditions and is quite tough, though not as hardy as privet. It clips well but grows very rapidly so that frequent attention is necessary. It has small box-like leaves and can be used for heights up to 4 feet or so, after which it tends to lose strength.

Holly that has been clipped.

Privet hedge.

PRIVET (*Ligustrum ovalifolium*)

Privet has been much maligned due to its well-known prevalence in towns and suburbs where it is to be seen as the most popular hedge variety. Although not a striking plant to look at, it does in fact provide a very good hedge and is easily cultivated in any soil. Privet is used for topiary work as well as hedges, as many examples in this book will testify. It requires clipping a little more frequently than other varieties — two or three times a season — but is otherwise very tolerant and adaptable.

Two excellent examples of yew hedging.

Yew block hedge with dramatic decoration.

YEW (*Taxus baccata*)

The common yew is the favourite evergreen hedge for topiary growers, quite apart from its use for individual topiary specimens. Yew is not as slow growing as is often supposed (growth of up to 12 inches a year is not unusual) and ten years will see a respectable yew hedge looking fairly mature. It provides a tight crisp shape when clipped and its rich dark tone can be used to offset lighter plants or garden decoration such as statuary and urns. As an outer hedge defining a boundary, yew has to be used with caution in country areas because its leaves are toxic to animals (as they are to humans), but it is dense and forms a first-rate screen to the wind and weather.

Yew likes a well-drained soil but is a hardy plant with great longevity. If left to grow unchecked it can eventually reach 50 feet and is extremely strong. It can take severe clipping and, when it has been allowed to go out of shape by neglect, can be restored back to form by cutting back in careful sequence so that its former discipline is reattained in as thick and crisp a texture as before. There are a few pests and diseases which affect yew but these can be dealt with by spraying or clipping. On the whole yew gives little trouble to the gardener on the grounds of health, but it does not like sooty town atmospheres.

HEDGE PLANT CHART

	Purpose	Soil tolerance	Position	Planting time	Space apart		Clipping time	
					inches	centimetres	during growth	when established
Deciduous plants								
Beech (*Fagus sylvatica*)	Boundary, tall	Most, well drained Excellent on chalk	Town or country	October – March	18	45	August	August
Hawthorn (*Crataegus monogyna*)	Boundary, tall	Most	Anywhere except seaside	October – March	12	30	June and every 6 weeks	July/August
Hornbeam (*Carpinus betulus*)	Boundary, tall	Most well-drained	Town or country	October – March	18	45	August	August
Privet (*Ligustrum ovalifolium*)	Boundary, tall	Most	Town or country	October – April	15	37	June and every 6 weeks	May and September
Evergreens								
Box (*Buxus sempervirens*)	Low, decorative	Well-drained including chalk	Town or country	April – May	18	45	June and every 6 weeks	July/August
Holly (*Ilex aquifolium*)	Boundary, tall	Most	Windy, sooty	April – May	18	45	June and every 6 weeks	August
Lonicera (*Lonicera nitida*)	Low	Most, including moist	Anywhere	April – May	15	37	Frequently as required	Monthly May – August
Yew (*Taxus baccata*)	Boundary, tall	Well-drained	Not town as polluted	April – May	18-24	45-60	June and every 6 weeks	August
Conifers								
Lawson cypress (*Chamaecyparis lawsoniana*)	Boundary, tall	Most	Anywhere	April – May	24	60	Lightly to shape	August
Leyland cypress (*Cupressocyparis leylandii*)	Boundary, tall	Most	Anywhere	April – May	24-30	60-75	Lightly to shape	August
Monterey cypress (*Cupressus macrocarpa*)	Boundary, tall	Most	Anywhere including seaside	April – May	24	60	Lightly to shape	July/August
Thuja (*Thuja plicata*)	Boundary, tall	Most but lime-free	Anywhere including windy	April – May	24	60	Lightly to shape	August

View from balustraded retaining wall of topiary 'buttresses' and cones at Balcarres, Fife.

Planting a hedge

Site preparation

Clearly, the size of the site will depend upon the space available, but there are certain important points to note:

Keep the design simple.

Full sunlight is essential both for the vigorous growth of the hedge and for the topiary in the garden.

The proposed garden area should be as flat as possible.

A square or rectangular area is best.

Map out on paper the position of paths, walks and flowers beds, as well as access to and from the garden.

Some kind of viewing point is desirable in a topiary garden. Perhaps the easiest, if possible, is a raised terrace on the north side. The sunlight necessary for growth of the garden will not be affected but there would be an excellent vantage point from which to appreciate the design. One of the best views of Levens Hall garden, which does not have a raised terrace, is from the upper windows of the house.

A marvellous example of boundary hedges in yew at Crathes Castle, Aberdeenshire.

Soil (see also next section)

The soil in which to plant hedges should consist ideally of good quality loam, thoroughly prepared and capable of maintaining the trees for at least a lifetime.

Digging and manuring *must* be done if the conditions are not reasonably good.

Always remove turf and all weeds before planting. Chemicals can be used for this purpose but the manufacturer's instructions must be followed. A more old-fashioned method is that of hoeing, shallow digging and spot weeding.

If there are no strong perennial weeds on the site, the turf which has been removed can be laid upside down beneath a spade's depth of topsoil. Turf inverted in this way provides excellent growth material.

To assist drainage if the soil is heavy clay, a land drain consisting of a porous clay tube or pipe can be placed at the bottom of the trench and covered with rubble. The manure, turf and soil can then be placed on top of the tube.

A young thuya hedge.

Godington Park, Kent. A formal enclosure of hedging in which the corners are emphasised by the use of the square 'pillar-box' obelisks; these add solidity and a feeling of permanence to the design.

Above, a yew hedge at Hever Castle, Kent, with structural 'buttresses' which add great power to the design and which frame the flower beds in protective fashion. Left, monumental yew hedging at Great Dixter, East Sussex.

A spectacular, massive battlemented hedge at Knightshayes, Devon.

Hedge in Hampshire enclosing a formal garden.

Arcaded privet hedging at Green Animals, Rhode Island.

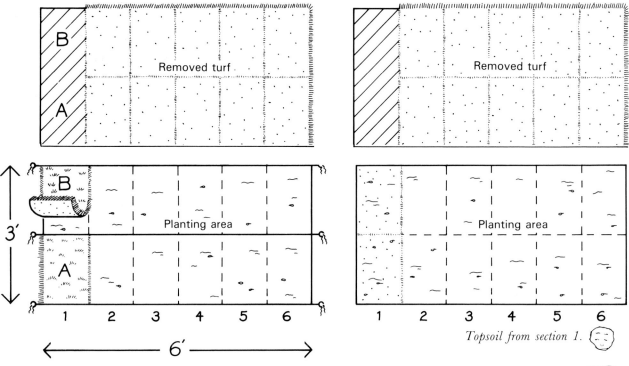

Figure 1. Removal of turf.

Figure 2. Digging sequence.

Topsoil from section 1.

Undersoil from section 1.

The drawing in Figure 1 shows the planting area 3 feet wide by 6 feet long marked out by stakes and cord. The turf has been removed from sections 2-6 and placed in readiness upside down at one side of the trench. The last two turves (A and B) are to be removed and placed in the shaded area shown. This will leave the whole area ready for digging.

The drawing in Figure 2 illustrates the digging sequence described on this page.

How to prepare the soil for a hedge

Decide on the position of the hedge. Mark out the area accurately with bamboo stakes and taut cord. Remember that 3 feet is the minimum width suitable, otherwise the plants will have to compete with surrounding turf, plants and weeds.

Begin by removing the turf, if it exists, with a turfing iron or spade. If the turf is clear of perennial weeds reserve it on one side of the proposed planting strip.

Prepare a section at a time, starting at one end of the area. The diagrams above show (Figure 1) the removal of turf and (Figure 2) the digging sequence with the area divided into 6 strips, each 3 feet wide.

From the first strip (Figure 2), with the turf already laid aside, remove the topsoil, i.e. the top 2-3 inches of soil, and place this at the end of section 6, on the opposite side of the trench to the turf. It will be needed for the final section.

Now dig out the first section (1) to one spade's depth, putting the removed undersoil close to the topsoil you have placed at the end section (6) but keeping the two carefully separate. This soil will also be needed to fill the final section (6).

Cover the whole of the bottom of the trench with inverted turf — if no turf is available, use manure or well-rotted compost.

From the adjoining section — 2 in Figure 2 — skim off 2-3 inches of topsoil and place this on top of the inverted turf or manure in section 1. Now dig out section 2, spreading the undersoil evenly over the inverted turf and topsoil in section 1.

You now have an empty trench in section 2. Place inverted turf in it, then the topsoil and the undersoil from section 3 to fill section 2. Continue in this way until you reach section 6, when you use the reserved topsoil and soil from section 1. Fork over the area to break down any lumps and make it level.

This preparation is best done at least a month before planting. Add a compound fertiliser to the topsoil before planting at the rate of 4 ounces to each strip.

Pointers for planting hedges

Planting near pathways and flower beds.

Allow for the plant's width when it is mature — the hedge should not be less than 3 feet wide.

 Always measure out the width of the mature hedge. Then mark out the centre line with stakes or a cord — this will give the future middle point of the hedge. Plant on that line. In this way you will avoid the situation where the hedge comes to overlap the path when mature.

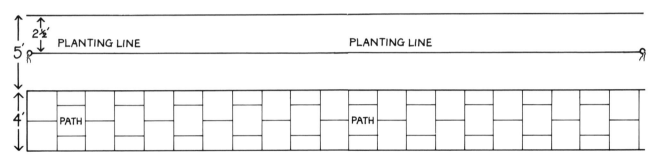

For example, if a plant grows to 5 feet wide, then the planting line should be 2 feet 6 inches from the path.

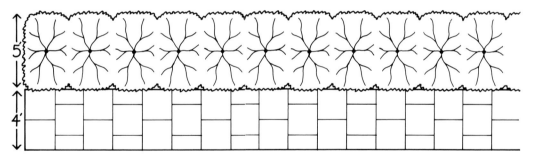

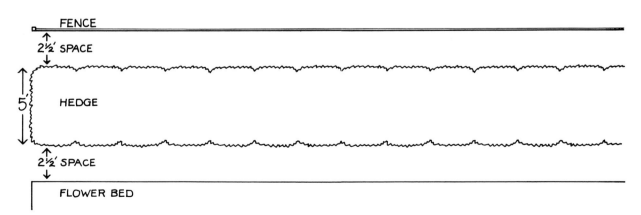

Remember to allow access for maintenance of the hedge.

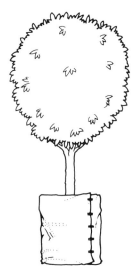

Container-grown plant.

A leylandii hedge.

Buying and planting hedges

Choose plants which have been grown in your local area as they will be acclimatised to local conditions.

Always buy your plants from a reputable nurseryman.

Make sure that they are all of the same height when you buy them.

Plants can be bought either: container grown — these can be planted at any time of the year; or dug out of the ground and root balled in sacking — these are usually planted in spring; or as bare-rooted plants — most deciduous plants are available bare rooted when in the dormant stage. Roots are usually covered in plastic with no soil. Plant in late winter or when soil thaws.

Directions for planting once the trees have been obtained

When the plants arrive try to get them planted as soon as possible. If there is going to be a delay then remember:

Root-balled plant.

Container-grown plants should be kept watered, placed in a shady, wind-free place until planted.

Root-balled plants with sacking wrapped round the roots should be kept watered and stacked together for support. They should also be kept in a shady, wind-free place until planted.

Bare-rooted plants should be heeled in a shady position, i.e. put in a shallow trench and covered by moist peat or soil. If the plants are tall, lean them at an angle so that they are supported by the ground. They should be kept watered and planted out before the root growth starts.

Planting container-grown plants

Prepare the site as shown on page 34. Plants being positioned less than 3 feet apart are best put in a trench.

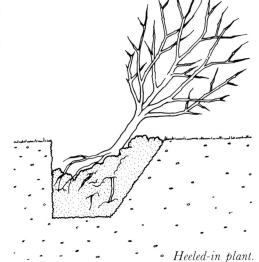

Heeled-in plant.

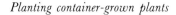

Bare-rooted plant.

36

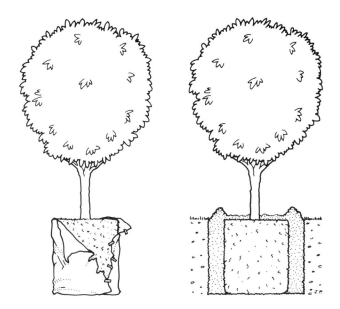

Potted holly plant.

Remove container carefully and place plant in middle of trench or hole.

Otherwise prepare holes for planting.

Water the plants well if they are found to be very dry.

Remove the plants carefully from the containers to avoid damage.

If the roots are contorted and circle the root ball, tease them out carefully and cut them off so that they will spread once planted.

Place the plants in the middle of the trench or holes, spacing them evenly by means of a marked stick.

If planted in a very windy area it is a good idea to stake each plant with a bamboo stake until they have become firmly rooted. Remember to tie loosely.

Fill in the trench or holes with soil and firm down.

Remember not to fill over the original soil line, which can be clearly seen on the stem of the plant. The soil line is indicated by a lighter or darker line on the stem.

Make a slight depression around the plant in a circle so as to make a 'basin' for the water when you water the plant in.

Water well, allowing the soil to settle and adjust the height of the plants if necessary. A mulch can be applied evenly over the root area, but take care not to make this too thick otherwise it will prevent moisture from reaching the roots.

Young box plant.

Deciduous hedging — beech at Hole Park.

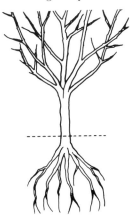

Bare-rooted plant showing soil line.

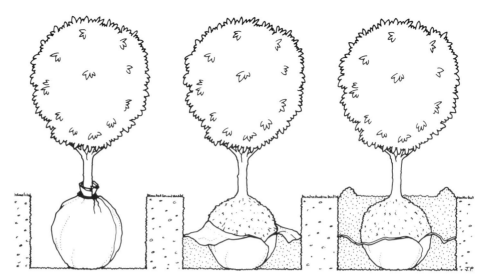

Place root-balled plant in prepared hole or trench.

Fill hole around plant to halfway up ball. Untie sacking and loosen around ball above soil. Lay neatly over added soil.

Continue to fill hole — firming down over loose sacking. Finally when hole is filled firm down and water. Adjust soil level when it has settled.

Planting root-balled plants

Have the site ready and prepared. Root-balled plants may be planted either in a trench or in holes, as with container-grown plants.

Place plant carefully in its trench or hole and adjust the height so that the soil line will be in the correct position when the trench or hole is filled with soil.

Untie and fold back the sacking round the roots. Do not remove it completely unless it has been treated to resist rotting.

Cut off any excess sacking from the sides and then put back the soil to fill the hole or trench, firming it down by hand or with a spade until it is level with the surrounding earth.

Form a water basin by making a circular depression round the plant as with container-grown plants and water the plant well. Allow the soil to settle and then adjust the level if necessary.

Apply a layer of mulch, again not too thick because a thick 1-2 inch layer will prevent moisture from penetrating to the plant.

A hedge made more interesting by magnificent arching. Brome Hall, c.1900.

38

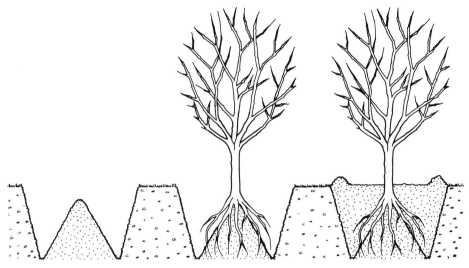

*Cone-shaped mound of
soil in hole.*

*Bare-rooted plant placed
over mound. Roots are
spread evenly over soil.*

*Fill space around plant
with soil, firm down and
water.*

Planting bare-rooted plants

Have the site ready and prepared.

Dig a hole wide and deep enough to accommodate roots without crowding.

Make a cone-shaped mound of soil in the centre of the hole. Add a firmly-positioned stake if the area is liable to strong wind.

Place the plant over the mound taking care to spread the roots out evenly.

Check the height against the soil line and adjust accordingly.

Add soil around the roots to back fill and firm down.

Water deeply to settle the roots.

Adjust the soil and plant level once the soil has settled.

Apply mulch as for root-balled plants.

A group of plants in modern packaging.

Bare-rooted beech plants heeled into soil.

Detail of leader shoot on thuja hedge.

Care after planting

After hedge plants have been installed in the ground it is advisable to follow certain rules in order to obtain the optimum results.

Deciduous hedges

Naturally upright-growing species such as hawthorn and privet should be cut back hard after planting. At Wisley, the Royal Horticultural Society recommend that they are cut back to 4 to 6 inches above ground level, while other authorities suggest 6 to 8 inches, so this very severe treatment has considerable support. The effect is to encourage vigorous growth during the first season. In the second year, fairly severe pruning is again recommended, even back to 6 inches of the base of the younger wood.

Naturally bushy growers such as beech and hornbeam need not have quite as severe a pruning initially as the upright growers. The leading shoot and longer side growths should be cut back by one third of their initial length.

In the second year similar treatment will prevent the hedge from growing too tall and will make for a good base.

Evergreen

Evergreens such as yew and conifers have a naturally dense and bushy habit. In the first year they require no early pruning apart from light clipping to contain straggly branches which impair the shape. The leader shoot should not be cut until the hedge has reached the required height, so it will be some time before this is necessary.

In the meantime the sides of the hedge should be clipped to keep it narrow and the plants should be fed and watered to encourage the leader to grow. Yew is typical of this type of plant and responds to this treatment very well.

Young thuja hedge.

Levens — clipping of lower level plants. Hedging shears are an essential tool for topiary shaping and maintenance.

Clipping of hedges during growth period

General instructions for hedge clipping

The main purpose of clipping hedges during their early growing period is to help form a close, dense base. To make sure that this happens they should not be allowed to increase in height too rapidly. During these early years, about three or four clippings a year may be necessary, whereas a mature hedge will not need more than one or, at most, two clippings a year. With hedges such as box, yew, holly, hawthorn and privet, clipping should be started in June and repeated at about six-week intervals. Beech and hornbeam should be clipped in August. Once a hedge is mature and has reached the height required it should be clipped in late summer, i.e. August or early September. See table on page 29 for the clipping times.

Clipping principles

Always use sharp tools, whether they are shears or electric hedge trimmers, for all species of plants. It is normally recommended that large-leafed evergreens such

Some of the most useful tools for clipping hedges — pruning saw, secateurs, electric hedge trimmers and shears.

Two examples of ladders used for trimming hedges.

An example of good cone shapes decorating the top of a hedge.

as laurel, bay and holly be clipped with secateurs to avoid leaf damage but this is very demanding as far as time is concerned.

Check ladders, if they are to be used, to make sure they are safe.

Early in the year and after the frost is the time to clip if strong growth is needed — in England this is usually between March and April, and clipping at this time can be done to create new growth if a plant is in the formative stage or if it is to be cut back strongly to reshape it. The plant will have time to recover and grow before next winter.

Remember that rounded or curved lines are much easier to cut than straight lines or flat surfaces, which may need some guidance by means of plumb lines or similar straight edges to work to.

The following illustrations show the best cross-sectional shapes for hedges.

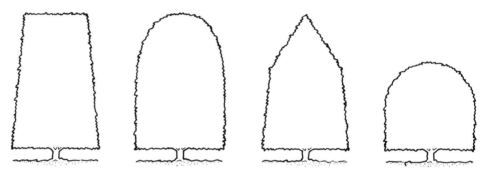

Good shapes for hedge sections — following natural progress of plants. Sunlight and moisture obtained at an optimum, snow will not collect and any damage will be reduced.

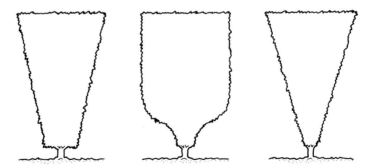

Cross sections which do not follow natural progress of plants. Such shapes will only give poor growth in areas out of sunlight and are liable to be damaged by snow.

Hedge at Knights-hayes, Devon, used to create a structural background and alcove for statuary, charmingly offset by the formal lily pond.

Internal hedging at Hever Castle, Kent, showing a well-clipped arch. Here, the hedge creates a 'room' within the overall garden.

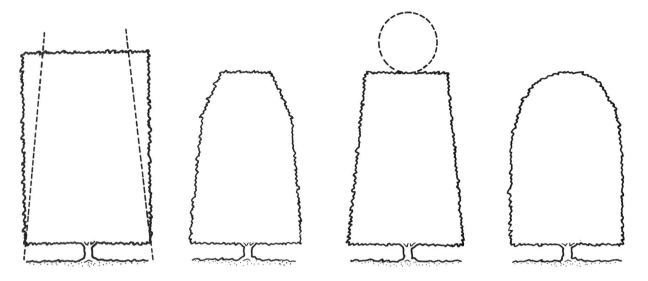

Dotted line indicates the angle of the batter.

Various types of hedge batter, the first being excellent for subsequent additional decoration.

Hedge batter

The batter is the slope of the hedge away from the vertical. Having such an incline or batter has two advantages — it makes the hedge look substantial, and it allows the hedge to receive sun and air at the bottom where it should be kept dense.

The ideal batter for a hedge is obtained by an incline away from the vertical of 2 to 4 inches for every foot of height.

A well 'battered' hedge at Wisley.

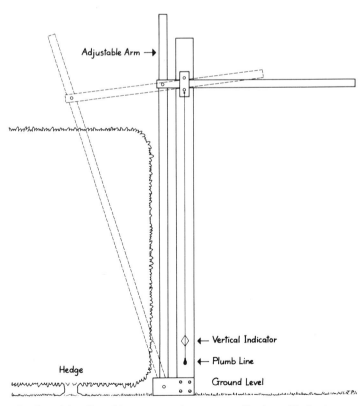

Device with adjustable arm to assist accurate clipping of hedge batter. The guide for the adjustable arm is marked out with a scale to give the relevant batter. (See page 48 for photographs of device in use.)

Massive hedge with arched piercing and portholes which give effects of light and shade to the overall solidity. Sudeley Castle, Gloucestershire.

Clipped hedges acting as link between architectural piers at Gayhurst, Buckinghamshire.

Superb topiary work at Brockenhurst Park, Hampshire. The arches are well proportioned and ideal for displaying statues or as windows.

Maintenance — established hedges

To keep a good hedge

Prune it regularly.

Fertilise it with a slow release fertiliser.

Cut out any diseased or dead wood and tie back any branches that distort the outline.

Do not clip when there is a danger of frost. Brush off snow as the weight can damage specimens.

To renovate a hedge that has become neglected

Most worn-out or neglected hedges can be renovated by forcing new growth.

Clipping or pruning in spring will stimulate new growth and can thus be used to repair any damage.

Bare spots can be filled in by replacing dead plants.

Broad-leafed evergreens should be renovated in early spring.

Deciduous hedges should be renovated during the dormant season.

Few coniferous needled evergreens respond to severe pruning. If they are cut below current leaf growth the plants of this type will not respond.

Decoration can always be added to the simplest shape, i.e. piers, pilasters or square crenellations. Simple spheres and domes, topping piers or plinths at entrances or gateways provide splendid formal emphasis to these features.

Three methods of achieving an accurate cut when trimming established hedges

Tools needed include sharp shears or electric hedge trimmer, stakes, string or mason's cord, spirit level.

1. To cut horizontals using mason's cord or string:

Decide on the height of the hedge.

Drive a 2 inch stake into the hedge through the branches close to the side

A fine example of horizontal cutting of clipped yews, showing the Egyptian doorway and sphinxes at Biddulph Grange, Cheshire.

surface; the stake should project above the top level of the hedge.

Complete the staking by placing stakes at 6 foot intervals until the end of the hedge is reached.

To check that the level is correct place a board between the stakes and then, using a spirit level, check the continuous levels.

When satisfied with the levels, remove the plank and spirit level.

Measure from the top of the stakes down to the required height of the hedge, mark each stake and then tie a cord between the marks. If the cord dips in the middle, prop it up with an extra stake.

This cord may now be used as a guide for the cutting.

If the hedge is wide, cut half the hedge and then repeat the procedure on the other side. It will be relatively easy to cut accurately between the two sides.

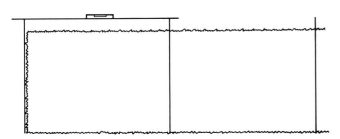

Horizontal clipping — stakes and board with spirit level in position.

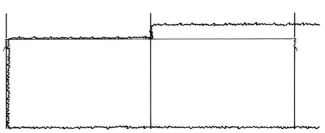

Horizontal clipping — cord tied at required height and first section shown clipped.

Cutting a vertical using batter device.

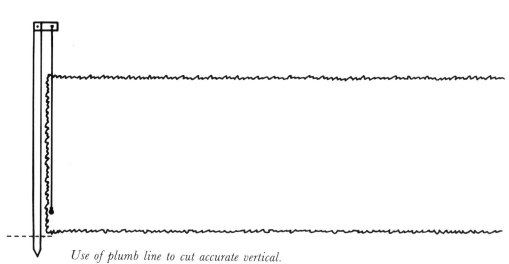

Use of plumb line to cut accurate vertical.

Batter device with adjustable arm set away from the vertical.

2. To cut an accurate vertical line using a plumb line:

This is simple to make using a stake with a small piece of wood nailed across the top. Drive a nail into the end of the small piece of wood, then tie a piece of string to the nail. Make the string long enough to hang almost to the end of the stake. At the end of the string add a weight.

Fix the stake in the ground against the edge of the hedge, with the string just touching the hedge. When the line is steady and remains still, cutting can begin using the string as a guide.

3. To cut sloping sides on a hedge using a batter device (the most accurate way to cut sloping sides):

Batter device in position.

Use angled arm as cutting line.

Last but not least — a large piece of plastic sheet can be laid on the ground beside the hedge to catch the cuttings and thus save a lot of back-breaking time collecting the cuttings after the hedge trimming is complete.

To cut windows and portholes

Mount a template on a stake which can be driven into the ground. Avoid main stems or trunks of plants by cutting between them. A wire or metal frame can be made to support the shape as in the Sissinghurst hedge (bottom left).

A porthole cut in the hedge at Sissinghurst, Kent.

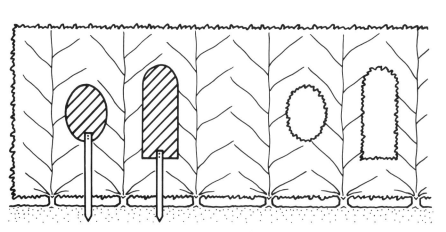

Templates on stakes are used to cut windows and portholes.

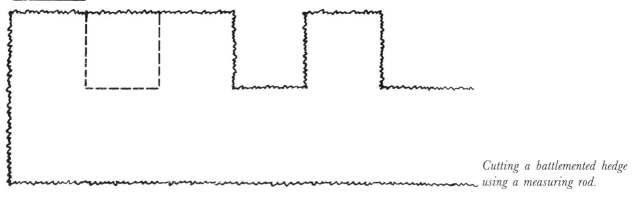

Cutting a battlemented hedge using a measuring rod.

To cut battlements

Decide what lengths you want and use a measuring rod to measure out the crenellations. If all the cut-outs are square, one rod provides all the dimensions.

To cut decorative shapes in the hedge top

To achieve a symmetrically-shaped hedge top, use a template on a stake which can be driven into the ground. The overlap should give the correct space of the shape.

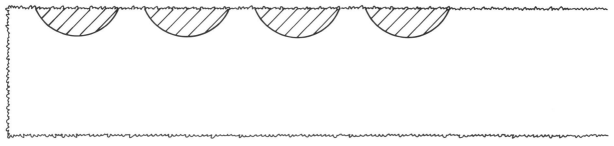

Proposed shaping of hedge.

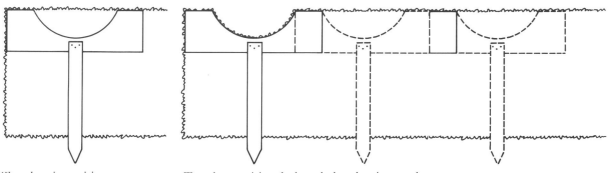

Template in position.   *Template positioned along hedge showing overlap.*

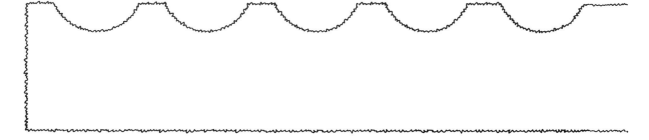

Hedge accurately cut.

Imaginative topiary shaping.

Chapter Four
TECHNIQUES OF
TOPIARY PRODUCTION

Cloud shaping at Meadowbrook, Virginia, U.S.A.

Another decorative example of potted topiary.

Plants for topiary

A wide variety of trees and shrubs can be shaped. In Japan the shaping and training of trees is an ancient art formulated on a highly sophisticated sense of design. Topiary of the kind we are dealing with in this book, however, comes of a European tradition which has been enthusiastically adopted by Americans and which has confined itself to a reduced number of species for reasons of suitability, control and economic practicability. Plants used for topiary work need to be hardy, to withstand sharp clipping over a long period and to grow densely and steadily but not too quickly, otherwise the labour of maintenance becomes excessive. In practice, therefore, the list of suitable species is usually much reduced from the total list of possibilities. On page 53 we illustrate a golden elm which has been clipped into a high spiral in a garden in Holland; at Disneyland, in Florida, the gardeners of those exuberant animals in high colours have added many new imaginative ideas to the production of attractions in all sorts of plants and flowers. Golden elm and these new species are not to be found in the list of suitable plants in this chapter, however; we merely show them to make the point that there are many trees which can be adapted to popular forms. Those shown below are simply the ones which have been found most suitable over a long period.

BAY (*Laurus nobilis*)
Sometimes known as the sweet bay, *Laurus nobilis* is said to be the original of the laurel used in ancient times for wreaths and crowns of honour, although this has also been claimed for the myrtle. There is no connection between the *Laurus nobilis* and the common laurel, which is a variety of prunus. The bay is a hardy evergreen shrub with aromatic leaves. It likes full sunshine and will grow in any normal soil but should be sheltered.

For small topiary work the bay is much to be seen in tubs, as a standard 'Berlin stem' type of design with a ball of leaves above a bare stem. It is also clipped into other formal shapes suitable for small gardens, courtyards or terraces.

BEECH (*Fagus sylvatica*)
Beech is principally used for hedging and is described in detail in Chapter 3, but many hedges used in topiary gardens are sculpted into architectural shapes, particularly large arches, through which suitable vistas can be seen. The problem with beech is that it tends to grow large and can require special equipment for clipping when it achieves great heights.

BOX (*Buxus sempervirens*)

If yew dominates the topiary kingdom, box follows it closely as a superior aristocrat, if not a major baron, ruling particularly strongly in America and Holland, even though the scale of topiary creations in box is often kept to a smaller scale than that of yew. Box provides a series of about seventy different species of evergreen shrubs which are slow growing and dense enough to make first-class topiary figures. It takes clipping without demur provided no frost is likely and, like yew, is tolerant of most soils. There are coloured and variegated varieties, as well as the dark-green common box of *Buxus sempervirens*, and all are suitable for topiary although the variegated variety tends to be too brittle for use in the contemporary Dutch topiary figures described in Chapter 8.

Box also likes drained soil and protection from strong winds. It can be grown from cuttings in a trench 6 inches deep or in beds as shown in Chapter 8. Cuttings are planted deep to encourage extra roots which will ensure that the specimens can be replanted without difficulty. To grow from cuttings of this sort to a bush capable of topiary shaping at about 3 feet high takes up to six years, but box will continue to grow much higher than this if desired and there are specimens illustrated in these pages which go well over 6 feet — the normal maximum is about 10 feet.

A frequent use of box is for the low hedging that borders formal flower beds and for this there is a dwarf variety, *Buxus sempervirens suffruticosa,* that is very suitable. It can be kept a few inches high by hard clipping and provides a useful means of maintaining the decorative structure of a garden's flower beds throughout the winter months. Box can be fed by the application of manure to the surface area around the bush since it is surface-rooting, but it can also be fed with fertilisers and liquid manure. It is attacked by box suckers, which feed on the sap of young leaves which fail to expand, and can be affected by leaf spot, rust and yellowing or browning of the leaves.

Box.

Conifers

JUNIPER (*Juniperus*)

Junipers provide a wide variety (about sixty species) of evergreen, bushy trees and shrubs which in many cases take a vertical, formal shape in themselves without much clipping. There are, however, irregular species and spreading or prostrate ones.

The best-known is probably the *Juniperus communis* or common juniper, which occurs in Britain and North America as a shrubby bush or small tree up to 10 feet high. It is suitable for exposed sites and for chalk with thin soil. There are dwarf forms of this, such as *compressa,* which grow to about 24 inches high.

Juniper.

LEYLAND CYPRESS (*Cupressocyparis leylandii*)
MONTEREY CYPRESS (*Cupressus macrocarpa*)
THUJA (*Thuja plicata*)

These three plants suitable for topiary are discussed in Chapter 3.

Thuya.

Country hedge with clipped holly tree.

Hawthorn hedge with shaped specimen tree.

Lonicera ball in the foreground with shaped leylandii behind.

HAWTHORN (*Crataegus monogyna*)

Hawthorn is perhaps more frequently used for hedging than anything else, but it can be and is used for topiary work and, although a deciduous plant, retains some of its leaves in winter. It likes the sun but grows in almost any soil and can be clipped without restraint. There are two hundred species of trees and shrubs in this genus, all normally with thorny branches. Hawthorn will grow in town pollution and in salty coastal winds.

Apart from *Crataegus monogyna,* the common hedge hawthorn, there are many specimen varieties which can be controlled into formal shapes, although the genus is not now as popular for topiary work as the evergreens.

HOLLY (*Ilex aquifolium*)

Here again is a plant perhaps more frequently used for hedging than for topiary work, but its rich dark evergreen colour can make it very striking when cut into a formal shape for the garden. It is very tough and can stand most soils, gales, town atmospheres and hard weather. It can be clipped very hard.

There are a hundred species, of which the *aquifolium* is the most common, being a tree which will grow 20 to 25 feet high. Golden and variegated varieties exist but variegated hollies will revert to green if neglected. Perhaps one of the most celebrated uses for holly in topiary is at Disneyland, where the famous animals make use, among other things, of three *Ilex* varieties — blue angel, opaca (east Palatka) and vomitoria (Yaupon holly) for such fauna as seals, elephants and even Mary Poppins.

HORNBEAM (*Carpinus betulus*)

Common hornbeam is another hardy species like beech and is used for hedging as well as for specimen trees. See Chapter 3.

LONICERA (*Lonicera nitida*)

Lonicera is a genus of some two hundred evergreen and deciduous shrubs and climbers which include the honeysuckle, the trumpet vine and woodbine. The Chinese honeysuckle, *Lonicera nitida,* is a dense evergreen shrub which can be used for hedging or for topiary. It grows well on most soils and in most conditions, taking wet soils such as clay in its stride. It clips well and forms excellently into shapes such as balls or spheres, but grows quite rapidly so that clipping is frequently required. Its leaves are small, dark green and lustrous. It will grow well up to about 4 feet.

Garzoni, Italy. A privet bird creation in the midst of the colourful profusion of a famous garden.

A spiral produced from a straight leylandii conifer whose need for a clip emphasises the rapid-growing character of this species.

A relatively young holly tree clipped into several tiers around its straight upright stem.

A spiral produced from a golden elm growing in a front garden in Holland.

Highly skilled use of privet in a Bristol garden.

PRIVET (*Ligustrum ovalifolium*)

Privet is much used in private fantasy and cottage topiary, inducing exuberant expressions such as the steam locomotive (left) and giraffe both shown in Chapter 5, but it would be wrong to dismiss this common plant as a mere provider of such amusements and of suburban hedges. There is much dignified topiary in privet and the formal gardens of Italy — see Chapter 5 and page 53 — have made plentiful use of this easily-cultivated plant. It is also the basis for the Green Animals garden of Rhode Island in the U.S.A.

There are about forty-five species of hardy deciduous and evergreen varieties of privet and its use is mainly for hedging, since it provides an ideal strong dark screen which thrives in urban conditions. The *Ligustrum ovalifolium aureum,* or golden privet, provides a tighter, slower-growing variety which is also very good for topiary work. More frequent clipping will be required for privet than for yew or box.

The *Ligustrum texanum* variety is used at Disneyland for topiary frogs, perching on the silvery *texanum* mushrooms.

Decorative use of two different species of yew. The golden dome is growing through the green base yew tree.

YEW (*Taxus baccata*)

At the top of any list for suitable plants for topiary must come the common yew (*Taxus baccata*), a native of Britain and to be found in its varieties (*aurea,* the golden; *pendula,* the weeping; *erecta,* the broom yew, etc.) in both Britain and the United States. It is faster-growing than is commonly supposed and can reach 5 feet within a few years from planting. After ten years yews will look considerably more mature than is usually believed and, if allowed to continue, will eventually reach a height of 50 feet. It is quite reasonable to expect an 8-foot tree after ten years of growing from a small nursery specimen.

Yews are hardy trees of great longevity and will withstand both drought and bitter winter weather. They like well-drained soils; water-logging of their roots causes the needle-like leaves to turn yellow or a coppery colour and to fall. Apart from this and an aversion to salt-laden winds they are tolerant of most types of soil including clay, chalk and limestone. Clipping can be carried out year after year without deleterious effects and, in the right conditions of sunlight, the yew forms a dense, compact tree which is ideal for the sharp definition of hard lines, edges and curves which are the sculptural hallmarks of really good topiary.

On the whole yew prefers a country atmosphere because polluted town air does not suit it, though it does have a measure of resistance. It must be used with caution as a hedge for bordering purposes in the country, however, because it is highly toxic to animals (and human beings); a separating fence may be necessary. Yew is attacked by scale insects which may encrust the stems, gall midges, and mites. It can also be affected by honey fungus which kills some of the roots though not necessarily destroying the entire tree.

Reams of laudatory literature have been written about the yew, from the Romans onwards, but proof of its kingship of the topiary world lies in the many and superb specimens of great antiquity which are still to be found adorning celebrated gardens the world over.

Basically simple shapes provide a varied collection in this large topiary garden at Heslington Hall, Yorkshire.

Shaping young trees and plants

Free shaping

While it is perfectly possible to buy a tree or shrub in a ready-made shape, as Chapter 8 shows in its description of contemporary Dutch topiary nurseries, a great deal of the fun of growing lies in creating your own shapes. The cottage gardener often has a good idea of the fancy to be created by simply looking at the tree or bush from every angle over a long period, but the planner of a new topiary garden needs some guidelines in styling the plants to his or her will. Having set out the plan, put in the plants and watched them start to grow, what should the topiary gardener do to ensure that they conform to the ambitious expectations originally conceived?

In general, like the garden plan itself, the principle of keeping things simple should apply to the shapes of the plants as well. The tree's natural shape and style of growth must be considered when selecting the form to be adopted. As a general rule, the ultimate shape should be apparent after about three or four years of clipping, bearing in mind that ideally a good year without clipping should follow after the planting described in Chapter 3. If the tree is part of a symmetrical garden plan involving, say, cones, pyramids or spheres, then there will be little need for difficult wiring or guiding by stakes, but more complex abstract sculptural shapes or animals will involve more careful thought and possibly the use of frames.

This group at Athelhampton, Dorset, shows simple basic forms which are still to be shaped at the top.

Another cubic base with ball above which is to be surmounted by further decoration.

A splendid specimen at Chilham, Kent, which is a development of simple, layered shaping. It is now slightly leaning with age.

This example at Godington Park, Kent, also shows simple layered shapes, but they are emphasised in this case by the separation of the tiers.

A line of topiary specimens at Chilham showing how basic shapes can be developed to dramatic effect.

Guide for free shaping young trees

Follow these simple principles when shaping without the use of frames:

Keep shape simple to start with.
Use tree's natural shape — do not fight nature too hard.
Keep shape broader at the bottom than the top — e.g. cones, pyramids, etc., are ideal.
Support with wire or bamboo stake if shape is more complex — do *not* constrict any stems by tying too tightly.
Always try to keep inside of bush clear and free of dead wood to allow light and circulation of air.
Birds or animals are shaped using pruning shears — cut, stand back — look — cut again!
Geometric designs and straight lines can be achieved by using string or cord as a cutting guide.
The advantage of a geometric design is that shapes can be added. For example, a cube formed in one to three years will form a cube plus cylinder in four to five years, will form a cube and cylinder with a bird on top in six to ten years.

The garden in Hampshire discussed on pages 96-99 is an excellent example of free-shaping topiary.

Starter shapes, using simple outlines

Good shapes to start with are the following:

Cone or pyramid
A cone is one of the easiest shapes to start with and follows the natural pattern of many trees. The great advantage of producing a cone is that it can be developed later into a more complex abstract or figurative shape by being used as the base of something grown out from the top leader shoot.

Spheres and cubes
These are also easy to produce at the start and can be developed later. Like cones and pyramids they are splendid formal shapes in themselves and can be used for the formal garden as part of a structural and proportioned plan, but they can also lead on to other forms of shaping.

These unclipped yew trees show how a squared base can provide the foundation for a severe formal shape which uses an architectural concept in topiary. The sprouting natural tops can be rounded off or domed according to taste or, more imaginatively, used as the basis for birds to cap the 'pillars' beneath.

These cylindrical shapes show how the natural growth of the yew tree can be modified to give attractive formal emphasis to an entrance or gateway in a hedge or garden.

A refinement of the cylindrical shape which makes further use of the natural shape of the tree.

These formal 'gateposts' show how square bases can be refined at the end of a hedge and capped with spheres or domes.

An uncut 'rough' shape which has great potential for formal clipping into a strong base capped by a sphere, cone or bird in the traditional topiary manner.

A remarkable shape from Hole Park, Kent, showing how the natural growth of the tree can be modified to give a striking layered effect.

An arched hedge gateway flanked by finials which could be used as a design for specimen topiary pieces. The natural upright shape of the tree is clearly identifiable.

Another much-used form which makes effective use of the tree's natural shape.

A bird mounted above crown and ball shapes, all on a single stem.

More sophisticated shapes

Circle

A circle requires a plant with two well developed side shoots on opposite sides of the main stems at the top of the tree.

Crown

To make a crown requires a plant or tree with four shoots growing out equally from the central stem at a coincident point or, at least, very close to one. The mistake is to assume that the shoots are bent upwards to form the crown: not so. The shoots should be bent *downwards* so as to use the tension of the tree itself and give a more resilient curve. Evergreen like yew or box is most suitable for this. Decide on the height of the finished crown before you start shaping.

A crown surmounting a formal cylindrical base.

A fine example of a circle topping a layered base at Levens Hall, Cumbria.

To form a circle:

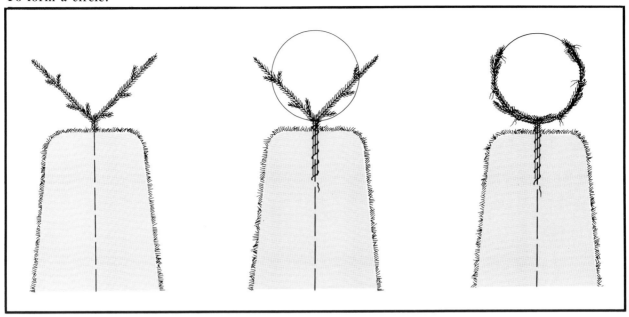

Allow two branches to grow from top of clipped base.

Carefully position a circular wire frame over the middle of base and tie to main trunk.

Tie the two shoots loosely to the circular frame. When they grow they will eventually form a circle which can be trimmed to keep it in shape.

To form a crown:

Allow the leader shoot to grow to approximately double the height of the required crown. Remove side shoots from leader leaving only four side shoots and leader shoot.

Take each side shoot, one at a time, and bend downwards towards the base of the crown and tie. Do the same with the other three shoots. Remember to space the shoots evenly.

You now have the basis of a crown which can be trimmed as it grows. The top of the leader shoot can eventually form a knob or ball.

To form a spiral:

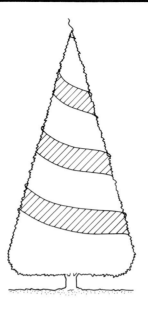

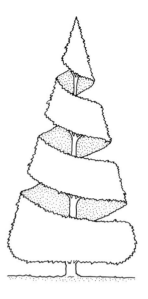

Tie a piece of string to the top of the cone-shaped tree. Wind it downwards in a spiral until you reach the bottom of the tree. The string should attach quite easily to the needles or leaves.

Starting at the bottom, using a pair of shears, cut a spiral following the string guide line. All leaves and stems should be removed right down to main stem.

The finished spiral should look like this. Obviously with time the outline will become sharper and more professional looking.

Spiral

A cone or pyramid shaped tree is ideal to start with, for instance one like that in the illustration below. Box is probably the easiest type of bush for first time shaping.

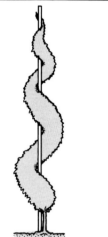

A slight cheat on an easy spiral: take a young supple pyramid-shaped plant. Drive a strong bamboo stake into the ground as close as possible to the stem. Gently wind the young plant around the bamboo. Tie if necessary. Eventually the shape will be maintained naturally and the stake can be removed.

The type of cone which can be adapted to a spiral as shown at the top of the page.

A completed spiral in box.

To form a peacock:

Allow at least five shoots to grow out from the top of your base, which can be a hedge or single specimen plant. Do not attempt shaping until the shoots are at least 2 feet high.

Divide the shoots, at least three for the tail, two for the body and head. The two head shoots should be pulled away from the tail to leave the tail clear for shaping.
Gently fan out the tail shoots, if necessary using wire to keep the shoots apart. Lightly trim to begin shaping the tail.

To start forming the body and head, loosely tie the two head shoots together. If the angle of body needs adjustment, a bamboo stake can be tied into the bush at the desired angle. The body and head are shaped around it. Use a small side shoot to form the beak. Tie lightly with wire or string, pull downwards and tie to body. See the peacock formation in Chapter 8 for detailed diagrams of this.

Peacock

Evergreen, like box, or yew will produce the most satisfactory result. This is not as complicated as it looks, but is such a traditional topiary shape that many people would like to produce it. Obviously, with a little alteration, you can change the type of bird quite easily once the general technique has been mastered. For example, the tail could be shortened or lengthened.

A quicker way to produce a topiary bird

The late eminent American topiarist, Admiral Neil Philips, suggests using two plants. In his nursery at Heronwood he grew *Buxus sempervirens* plants in hedges and singly.

To make a peacock he would combine a round single bush with a tall narrow plant from the hedge. The round plant produced the body, while the tall one became a tail. Planted one behind the other, with a little shaping, the job was already half done.

These yew birds share individual variations on the same theme, both using a solid cube for a base.

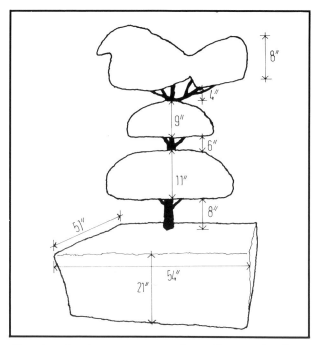

Drawing showing measurement of a well proportioned four-tier yew topiary, combining two simple shapes — sphere and rectangle — topped by a bird.

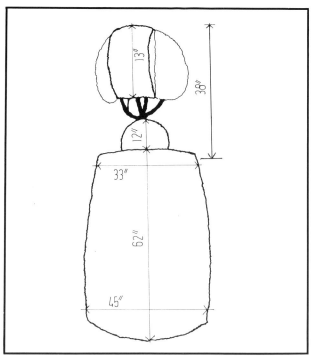

A diagram showing a simple cone, sphere and crown with relevant measurements.

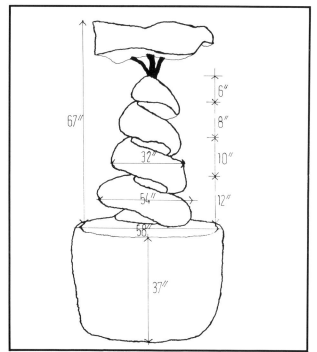

Simple base surmounted by spiral and topped by a bird in yew.

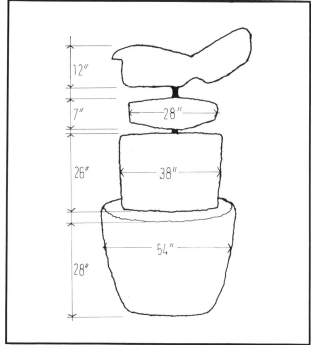

Another four-tier topiary in yew — simple, but with a strong feeling for design.

Six more advanced shapes

The six examples of specimen topiary (above, opposite and page 66) at Hever Castle are not difficult to shape if the instructions on shaping cones, spheres, cubes, crowns, spirals and birds are carefully followed. Of course many other variations are possible — great fun lies ahead for a potential topiarist.

Spheres on rectangular base, topped by a bird. Hever Castle. Dimensions opposite.

Crown on top of simple shapes. Hever Castle. Dimensions opposite.

This bird on a spiral and circular base is shown against the moat and castle at Hever. Dimensions opposite.

Another bird variation at Hever Castle, set on substantial base formed from cylindrical shapes. Dimensions opposite.

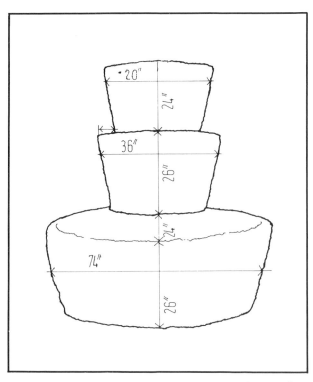

These receding cylindrical shapes or, perhaps more precisely, sections of cones, have been used to produce this powerful shape at Hever Castle.

Dimensional sketch of the previous example to show proportion.

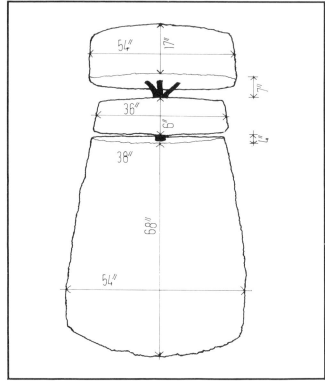

Another variation on cylindrical shaping at Hever Castle, showing the effect achieved by separation of the tiers.

Dimensional sketch of the previous example.

Three-dimensional wire frame of swan shape shown before use, either for a pot or mounting on other specimen.

Swan shape shown on top of a hedge at Ladew, Maryland. The body has grown in and the neck is in course of formation.

Outside metal-framed topiary

Many gardeners find it easier to create a topiary specimen from or around a strongly-designed metal frame. This technique is by no means new and, later in this book, examples are given of Brickwall, which provides a large-scale modern example, and Ladew in the U.S.A., as well as of Knightshayes in Devon. Both of the latter owe their inspiration to hunting, but any theme can be handled this way, allowing a frame of, for instance, a swan to be placed in position on a hedge or over a plant to ensure that it can provide the basis for training a plant to shape. The frame can be connected to another bush or hedge, or it can be free-standing as is the case at Brickwall described in Chapter 6. One of the advantages of using a frame is that it provides a good idea of the scale which is to be achieved in future — something not always easy to visualise when a plant is young and small.

In some cases a ready-made frame can be purchased from a specialist supplier, although this is much more likely in the U.S.A. than in England or other European countries. An alternative is to design a frame and have it made by a local blacksmith. If this option is chosen there are a few ground rules to be observed in designing a topiary frame and these can be summarised as follows:

Draw the outline of the shape desired, such as a bird, on a piece of card. Make it lifesize or bigger — a landscape can diminish the visual impact of an object. Use a thick felt pen and if you are not very good at drawing try and copy from a book or magazine and enlarge the drawing afterwards.

Take the design to a local blacksmith and get him to make the outline in metal and then fill in the shape with circles of framing to give the required three-dimensional effect. Remember that the form has to last, so make it rigid and strong.

Do remember to keep the outline simple. It will be easier to construct and the plant will be easier to keep in shape when it has grown in.

When the frame is completed ask the smith to add a stout metal rod to the frame which can be used to anchor it into the ground or to tie and fix it into a hedge, branch or stem.

As the plant grows, tie it to the frame so that the branches are evenly spaced. Once it starts growing through the frame you can start trimming, using the metal as a template. Remember to keep the inside as clear of leaves or needles as possible — the more air and light that get to the inside of the shape the better the specimen will be. Pull any new growth towards the outside and tie it to the frame. Occasionally there will be a need to trim and cut back inside if it gets too congested.

An outgrown yew hound being regrown on a new frame.

Example of frame used for hound in Ladew hunting scene.

The yew tree shoots clearly visible growing up from the hedge. These will finally form a hound at Knightshayes.

The outline shape of a swan formed by wire and joined by solder or wire.

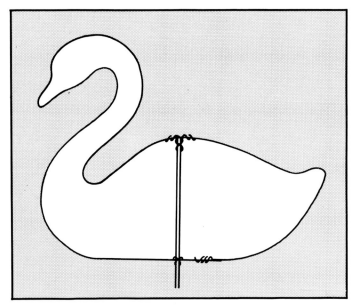

A metal rod is attached to top and bottom of the frame by wire. This rod will be used to anchor the frame over the plant and into the ground.

To make a simple swan frame:

If you want to make your own frame, the best procedure is to keep it as simple as possible. You will need:

Wire cutters.

Electric soldering iron or strong florists' tape or wire.

Galvanised wire which comes in 18, 16, 14, 12, 10 and 8 gauge (the lower the gauge the thicker the wire). No 8 gauge is considered the best for outside work and is fairly rigid.

All this equipment can probably be bought from an ironmonger, hardware store or do-it-yourself shop. Otherwise, try a building supply centre. If getting the wire is a problem, think about using wire coathangers.

How to begin

On to a piece of card draw the outline of your shape, always keeping it simple.

Use smaller, more pliable wire to start with, say 14 gauge.

Using the drawing as a guide, start at the bottom and follow the lines with the wire, bending it as your go until the shape is completed.

Leave an overlap of wire before you cut it so that the two ends can be joined securely, first with wire or florists' tape, then with solder if you intend to use this.

Attach a strong wire to the frame to use as an anchor to the ground or for tying to the stem of a plant.

Once a proficiency in shaping the wire has been achieved, you can then go on to three-dimensional frames, see opposite.

When the frame is completed, clean it thoroughly and rustproof it, following this with protective paint, preferably dark green in colour.

To make a three-dimensional swan frame:

A wire 'silhouette' frame of a swan — a simple shape to make with one join.

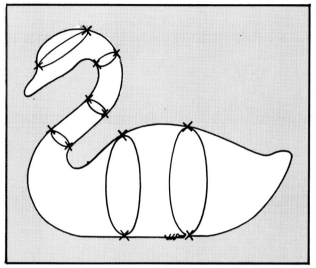

Circles of wire are placed in position to give a three-dimensional effect. Where they touch the outline frame they are soldered or wired into position.

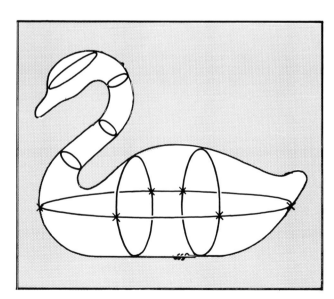

After the circles are fixed firmly into position the final bracing wire can be fixed to the opposite ends of the body. The fixing positions are shown as stars.

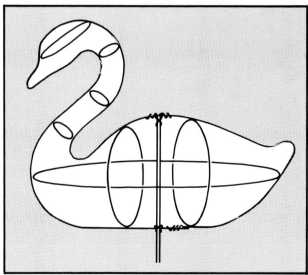

The frame is now complete — all that is needed is a strong metal rod attached to frame in two places which will enable the frame to be anchored in the ground or on top of a hedge.

A box peacock grown in a tub. This type of specimen has been shaped by the methods described in Chapter 8 on Dutch topiary.

Container growing of topiary plants

If you are given or you buy a shaped topiary plant from a nursery and wish to grow it in a container happily for a number of years, or if you dig an existing topiary out of your garden and wish to grow it in a tub, there are a few important considerations to bear in mind:

The tub design

The best types of tubs are made of woods such as oak, cedar, redwood, cypress or fir.

The ideal size of tub has inside dimensions 21 by 21 by 21 inches, but this could be difficult to find so you may have to have one made.

The bottom of the tub should have eight to twelve drain holes each approximately ¾ inch diameter.

The tub should have short feet or be raised on blocks to allow a 2 inch air space underneath.

The corners of the tub should be braced with angle iron to stand the weight and thrust of the plant ball.

A metal liner will add to the life of the tub but is expensive and heavy for ordinary handling. It must also be perforated.

A platform with wheels under the tub makes for easy moving when required.

How to plant a specimen into a tub

Place a good layer of broken crockery chips and gravel into the bottom of the tub to ensure good drainage.

Plants over 3 feet tall should have a tub of 21 by 21 by 21 inches inside dimensions. A larger tub becomes difficult to handle.

Over the broken crockery and gravel layer, place a light layer of soil.

Position the plant on top of the soil in the middle of the tub.

Loosen the sacking or protective fabric from the stem of the plant but not from the root ball — this wrapping will eventually rot anyway. If it is plastic remove it completely.

Fill the space around the root ball with plenty of light, loamy soil mixture, rich in humus, and enrich with bone meal.

Tramp this mixture down well to get rid of air pockets.

After firming down, the soil mixture should be about 4 inches below the rim of the tub.

Water thoroughly.

Add a layer of bark mulch to conserve and protect from heat and cold. This also looks neat and stifles weeds.

Keep the plant in shade for a week after it has been tubbed.

Water daily for the first week. Thereafter once a week.

All tubbed plants are best kept in partial shade for the first year. They should be protected from strong winds, kept away from dripping water, i.e. from the eaves of a house, and never stand in water or puddles. Always allow free drainage.

Do not fertilise the plant otherwise it will become gross. In a tub 21 by 21 by 21 inches give a big double handful of bone meal in autumn and a big double handful of dried blood in spring. Sprinkle the fertiliser on the surface and gently scratch it into the surface. Then water.

How to retub an existing specimen

Lay the tub gently on to its side.

Slide the plant out carefully, avoiding any damage.

Root prune lightly round the root ball to decrease its size. The aim of root pruning is to encourage the production of a well-established fibrous root system. Root prune in autumn rather than any other season.

To root prune, remove a tap root, if it exists, and any strong lateral roots with secateurs. This will encourage the fibrous roots near the stem and decrease the size of the root system.

If the retubbed plant has previously been left in too small a container, the curled and coiled roots should be cut. Long and tough roots should be pulled free and cut to loosen the ball. Do not let the root ball dry out.

Replace the plant in its tub and fill with new soil of a light, loamy type with added humus and bone meal. Firm down well and then water lightly.

Trim the leaves lightly; the plant will get a shock from the root pruning and this trimming will compensate for the reduction in stem growth.

Keep the plant in shade for a week after it has been retubbed.

Water daily for the first week. Thereafter once a week.

Three examples of container-grown topiary.

71

The management of established trees

In general, topiary requires fairly simple maintenance aimed at keeping the desired shape, repairing any damage and, occasionally, feeding the trees to encourage their health. It is as well to bear in mind that clipping diminishes the plant's ability to take in sustenance from the sun, so that late summer — August and even early September in England — is the favoured time for pruning or clipping. Of course, there are species which grow too quickly for shaping to be maintained by the ideal of one clipping per year and topiarists tend to love the neatness and order of the shapes they have created. There is, therefore, always a danger of overclipping.

The most potent danger to plants from clipping is that of frost, so it is very important not to clip when frost is likely. Box is particularly susceptible to frost damage.

Clipping or pruning in spring will encourage growth and should be used for neglected or damaged specimens requiring repairs. Topiarists argue about the use of hand or electric shears but there is no evidence that one is superior to the other and the maintenance of large areas of topiary becomes an enormous amount of work if all carried out by hand, so one can be guided accordingly. Larger leafed trees such as holly or laurel should, if possible, be cut by secateurs so as to reduce damage to the leaves.

See Chapter 3 for detailed clipping instructions.

Clipping time at Levens Hall — trestle ladders used for higher specimens.

Electric shears being used by the head gardener at Hever Castle to clip the specimen shown on page 66.

Buxus sempervirens suffruticosa being clipped by hand at Levens Hall. The low box hedges require similar maintenance to the large specimens.

Damaged specimen of yew at Great Dixter, severely cut back to encourage new growth.

Trestle ladders with planking used for high arch at Levens.

Chapter Five

WHIMSICAL SHAPES

A charming door decoration from Oxfordshire.

Anyone attempting to produce a controlled, trained shape from a bush, plant or tree has to have a certain concept in mind, a design, a fancy or a motif which they want to stand in their garden as a statement of some sort. The topiarised plant is a type of sculpture. Its placing, its form, its impact and its impression on the visitor all say something about its owner just as surely as sculpture in stone, bronze or wood utters a similar expression. The variety of shapes which can be made from plants is limitless; there is virtually no restriction which can be imposed apart from surgery which threatens the life of the plant itself. This being so, and human expression being what it is, topiary shapes of every kind can be found and can be created. They are not by any means always part of a formal scheme such as the dedicated garden planner would envisage. By far the majority of topiary figures are individual fancies in individual gardens. Some are there for us to admire reverently, some are there for us to smile at. Some are copied from patterns in famous gardens, some have evolved and been developed as the plant has grown. Some reflect an obsession with subject matter on the part of the owner. All are the result of proud cultivation, creative work and loving care.

An interesting topiary facade in Hampshire.

A well-sculptured bird in yew at Mount Ephraim, Kent.

74

A cottage group including a yellow canary at Kidlington in Oxfordshire.

Many variations have developed from the typical shapes used in traditional topiary work of the Golden Age. It is perhaps fair to say that yew seems to inspire the most formal approach to shaping, that box still encourages formality but leads to whimsy in the modern Dutch manner, and privet seems to excite fantasy on a lavish scale. Certainly the examples given here, whilst overlapping in some respects, tend to reinforce this impression. The examples shown here and on the following pages are, of course, only a selection of the vast variety that is to be found all over the world, but they do give an excellent indication of the great adaptability of plants to shaping, as well as of the imagination and inventiveness of both professional and amateur topiarists.

Abstract and animal-shaped topiary at Mount Ephraim, Kent.

A more fanciful bird at Mount Ephraim.

A variety of formal and animal topiary specimens in yew, box and privet, culled from countries as far apart as the U.S.A., Britain and Italy.

This magnificent privet engine in a private garden near Bristol, England, stands in its leafy siding waiting for the power to move out into the roads beyond.

Right, a more distant view of the locomotive and gondola in the above garden. Many years of painstaking care and attention, allied to hard work, have gone into these creations.

Venetian romance in England. This privet gondola, its gondolier and passengers dream of a Bridge of Sighs far distant and in a much warmer clime.

A spherical topiary specimen produced from separate yellow and green privet plants.

The cemetery at Tulcan in Ecuador is known locally as the Green Sculpture and grows at 10,000 feet above sea level. The plants are cypress *Cupressus amazonica,* and were started as topiary, about twenty-five years ago, by Don José Maria Azuel Franco. There are various geometric forms, birds, and amazing anthropomorphic heads whose inspiration comes from pre-Columbian forms belonging to an ancient culture.

In 1984 the Ecuadorian Government declared the topiary to be a national monument — possibly the first topiary ever to be so honoured. The area has an equable climate with temperatures ranging between 43°F to 68°F (6°C to 20°C) and a well-distributed rainfall which suits the plants. Tulcan is a small town in northern Ecuador, quite near the border with Colombia, so it is difficult to visit. Those who do get there agree that the topiary is well worth it.

After publication of pictures of this garden in the Royal Horticultural Society's magazine, one gardener was so inspired that she has laid out an 'abstract' topiary garden. No doubt there will be many more.

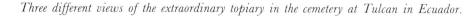

Three different views of the extraordinary topiary in the cemetery at Tulcan in Ecuador.

Above, a double row of topiary to celebrate the coronation of Queen Elizabeth II.

Below left, a guardian angel in a village churchyard and, right, an elaborately dressed lady from Bristol.

Above left, a box four-poster bed with vine creating the drapery; above, a pair of birds guarding their cottage at Sapperton, Gloucestershire; left, a well-draped box bench at Sissinghurst.

Far left, a strange little animal perched on one leg at Ladew; left, a sailing ship at Mount Ephraim; above, a father's teapot creation for his small daughter (now a middle aged lady!); below left, a huntsman with his hounds at Ladew; below, a delightful topiary bird on the road through Whatlington, Sussex.

The pyramidal yew avenue at Brickwall, c.1900.

Above and below, two views of Brickwall today.

Chapter Six
TWO GOOD GARDEN LAYOUTS

Brickwall, Sussex, and a garden in Hampshire

Many people who aspire to a garden in which topiary is used as part of the formal structure are put off both by the time scale and the planning elements involved. They feel, perhaps, that apart from the sculpturing of an existing tempting bush or small tree, the creation of a laid-out, formally-planned topiary garden requires a dynastic approach to gardening which is hard to envisage in our current, quick-fire, short-term, instant-installation times. This need not be so. Chapter 5 shows a variety of whimsical, formal, animal and other individual topiary pieces which can be created from existing bushes in isolation; this chapter illustrates two examples of planned gardens in which topiary plays an important overall role. Such gardens do not necessarily require three successive generations of gardeners to bring them to fruition. On the contrary, anyone taking the view that their current garden is likely to be theirs for ten years or more can draw on examples like these for ideas.

Metal-framed topiary

Brickwall, Sussex

The first example concerns the restoration of a more formal garden which was mentioned in Chapter 1. By a very appropriate coincidence the outer, neglected area of the original 'Dutch' garden at Brickwall, Northiam, Sussex, is currently being restored to produce a topiary garden with a chess theme and provides an excellent example of metal-framed topiary for the more ambitious and formally-inclined enthusiast to follow. Where the garden in Hampshire is a fine example of the sort of country garden which can be formally adapted with modest effort and planning, Brickwall is a fascinating model for the topiarist who has aspirations to a grander conception and is willing to produce the metal frameworks necessary for its realisation.

View of Brickwall's gardens and the pond, c.1900.

Brickwall: the old yews and the house today.

The walled gardens at Brickwall were laid out by Jane Frewen between 1680 and 1720, when the then unusual use of bricks gave the house its name. Plans of 1729 show that the basic layout of topiary, hedges and paths have survived today, even though in the nineteenth century the gardens were extended and the surrounding parkland laid out. For the last fifty years the estate has been used as a school and only routine garden management was possible so that the hedges and topiary had become overgrown. The walled garden was used for vegetables.

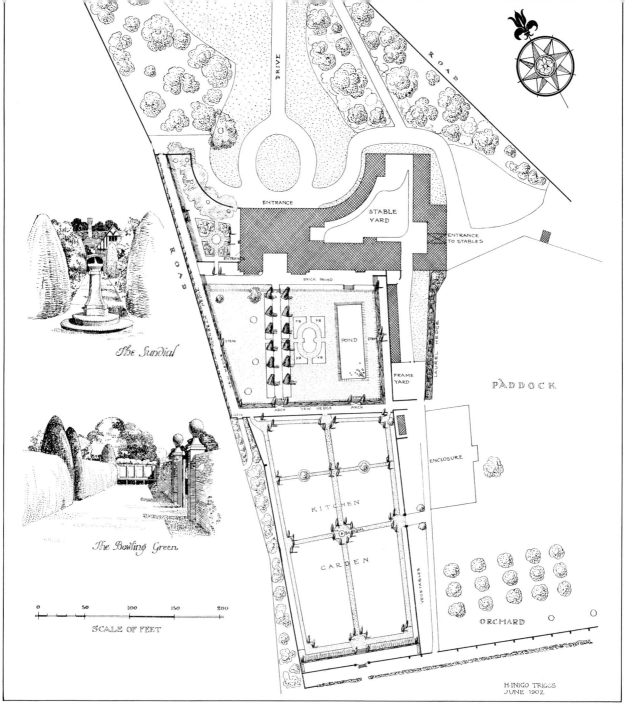

The Sundial

The Bowling Green

0   50   100   150   200

SCALE OF FEET

H·INIGO TRIGGS
JUNE 1902

*Above, plan of Brickwall's gardens as they were in about 1900. The formal conical yew walk
led to a transverse bowling alley or green between this section and the kitchen garden. Within
what had become the kitchen garden, Jane Frewen's groups of yews remained, showing the
remnants of the original structure. Left, detail of the conical yews in the yew walk.*

In 1979, however, with advice and grant aid from the Historic Gardens Trust
(Sussex), the restoration of the seventeenth century garden was begun by the
Frewen Educational Trust. The hedges and topiary have been pruned back hard,
new hedges planted, a border planted with species relevant to the period and new
trees put in the main approach to the house. The particular item of restoration
which is of interest to the aspiring topiarist, however, is the creation of the chess
garden to supplement the conical topiary walk of yew trees. This new garden has
been placed in the walled area beyond the yew walk and provides a superb

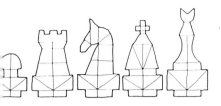

BRICKWALL
CHESS GARDEN

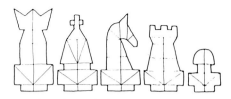

HE WALLED GARDEN –
hat was it like originally?

s not known exactly how Jane laid out this garden.

e first gardens were places for growing herbs for medicinal and usehold purposes, and fruit trees. By the Tudor period there was one garden but several: within these, herbs and salad plants re often grown in intricate decorative layouts. However, by ne's time, the formal garden with its geometric patterns was ite separate from the flowers and fruit.

ly three parts of the garden remain from Jane's time. The groups yews, strongly defining the junctions of the paths, may have en planted by Jane herself. The mulberry trees may be even lier: they came to England in the early 16th Century. The wling alley, at the end of the garden, may possibly be zabethan. (The garden water supply probably dates from torian times.)

PIARY – What is it?

piary is the art of clipping evergreens into artificial shapes. It kes use of plants in the same way that an architect would use ne or bricks: statuary or walls are formed from living material. w or box are most often used.

erest in topiary was at its height during the reign of William and ry, and it was also popular under Queen Victoria.

piary evolved from parterres which themselves derived from dor 'knots' – 'embroidering the ground with herbs'. Parterres re geometric designs of strapwork or arabesques in clipped ergreens and/or turf, planted on flat terraces. Sometimes the aces in the design were picked out with flowers or with coloured avel. The designs were flat and almost two dimensional, best preciated from upstairs windows.

ese evolved into the 'Dutch' style – green parterres of clipped k alone. The fashion was overwhelmingly for evergreens – pped hedges enclosed gardens and gravel walks. Punctuation given by exotic specimens such as orange trees which were ught out for the summer only, and by topiary work.

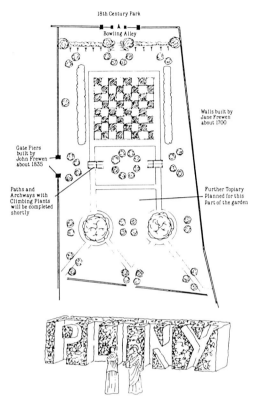

18th Century Park

Bowling Alley

Walls built by
Jane Frewen
about 1700

Gate Piers
built by
John Frewen
about 1835

Paths and
Archways with
Climbing Plants
will be completed
shortly

Further Topiary
Planned for this
Part of the garden

The first recorded topiary was in Roman Gardens

There are three main types of topiary:
(1) Abstract geometric shapes which form punctuation points or a group design.
(2) 'Architectural' hedges which enclose or divide but also step up or down or sport features such as archways or domes.
(3) Celebrated, or comic animal, figures.

The fashion for clipped evergreens had reached its peak in 1713 when Alexander Pope, the essayist, wrote his satiric catalogue 'Adam and Eve in yew: Adam a little shattered by the fall of the Tree of Knowledge, Eve and the serpent flourishing. Noah's Ark in holly: the ribs a little damaged for want of water. St. George in box: will be in a condition to strike the dragon by next April. Green Dragon of the same, with tail of ground-ivy for the present Edward the Black Prince in cypress. Divers eminent modern poets in bay, somewhat blighted …'

Soon after this was written the great landscape architects set the fashion for informality, and new styles of gardens came into being.

Today, topiary being one of the most ephemeral of the garden arts, few original examples remain. Old set pieces have grown huge and intimidating, instead of human-scale and intimate as the designers probably intended. Later examples of the architectural hedge can sometimes be seen as the background to herbacious borders. Many of the best examples of animal figures can now be seen peering over the hedges of small country gardens, basking in the attention of owner and passers by alike.

THE CHESS GARDEN –
Why make it?

New topiary, except for isolated instances in private gardens, is now a rarity. It was, however, characteristic of Jane's time, and so it was felt appropriate to form a new garden on this theme.

The Chess pieces on the board will eventually be formed of yew which will grow up inside the cages. The sides will be indicated by two foliage colours, dark green and golden.

All gardens are in a process of constant change, and the renewal of this one was begun only two years ago, in 1980. It is hoped that in due course the whole of the garden can be remade, and that you will come again to visit it as it grows to maturity.

Plan of the chess garden started in 1980. It shows the area encompassed by the kitchen garden of 1900 and the yews which still exist. The formal chess chequerboard has been laid out and the frames and pieces, with the yew plants, installed. Other improvements are planned for a later phase.

example of a modern effort to create an extraordinary topiary arrangement which would have done credit to any of the famous gardeners of the Golden Age.

By about 1900 the gardens at Brickwall conformed to a plan and the illustration opposite is a detail repeated from that plan. The kitchen garden still contained original yews which betrayed the first plan of 1680-1720, and it is this area which now contains the chess garden and which will have other improvements added later. The new plan of 1980, above, shows how carefully the Frewen Trust's architect, William Mount, Dip. L.A. (S.C.A.), F.I.L.A., has responded to the scheme and also shows the careful placing of the chess board. The basis of this board is a brick framing at ground level which contains alternate squares filled with dark and light gravel. The constructional drawing overleaf shows the architect's instructions for the building of the board which was carried out in conjunction with the East Sussex County Council and the Youth Opportunities Scheme. The dark squares use pre-coated bitumen on granite chips and the white squares use limestone chips; the effect can be seen in the photographs on pages 88 and 89.

Above, Brickwall as it is today; below, the garden front at the turn of the century.

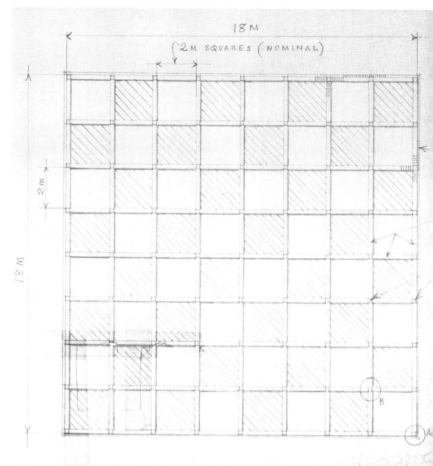

18M

('2M SQUARES (NOMINAL)')

2m

18 M

B

A

GENERAL LAYOUT PLAN 1:100

(POSITION IN GARDEN TO BE PEGGED
OUT BY E.S.C.C. STAFF)

PLAN 'B': TYPICAL
JUNCTION OF RIBS

William Mount's constructional drawing and instructions for the chessboard foundations, showing 6½ feet squares of alternately dark and light gravel chips contained in a brickwork ground frame.

BRICKWALL SCHOOL, NORTHIAM
CHESS GARDEN CHESS-BOARD CONSTRUCTION

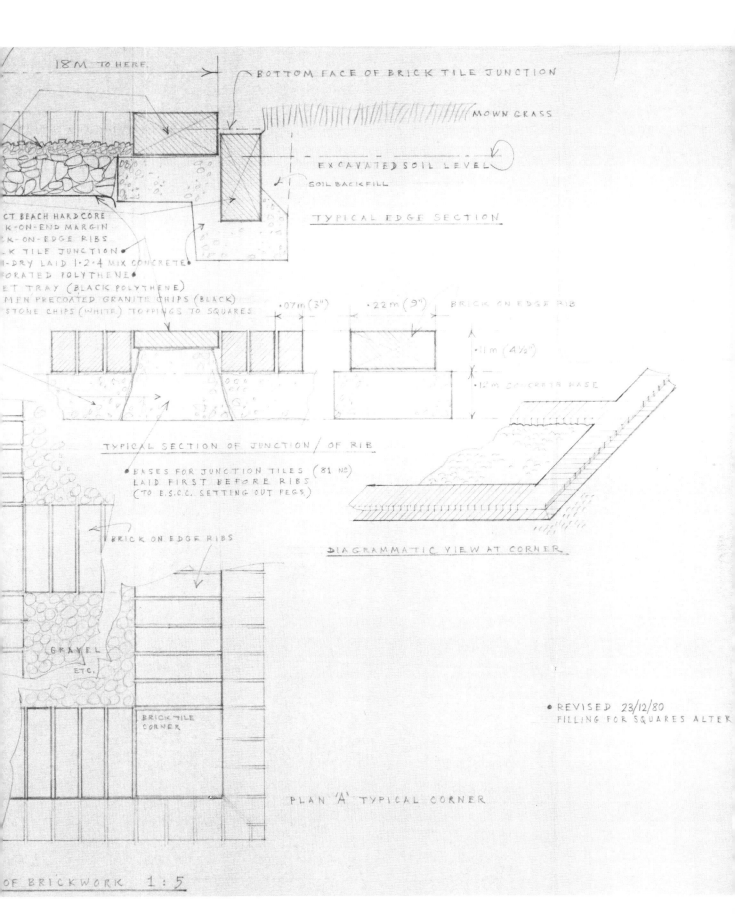

18M TO HERE.

BOTTOM FACE OF BRICK TILE JUNCTION

MOWN GRASS

EXCAVATED SOIL LEVEL

SOIL BACKFILL

TYPICAL EDGE SECTION

CT BEACH HARDCORE
K-ON-END MARGIN
CK-ON-EDGE RIBS
L-K TILE JUNCTION
M-DRY LAID 1·2·4 MIX CONCRETE
FORATED POLYTHENE
ET TRAY (BLACK POLYTHENE)
MEN PRECOATED GRANITE CHIPS (BLACK)
STONE CHIPS (WHITE) TOPPINGS TO SQUARES

·07m (3")   ·22m (9")   BRICK ON EDGE RIB

·11m (4½")

·12m CONCRETE BASE

TYPICAL SECTION OF JUNCTION / OF RIB

• BASES FOR JUNCTION TILES (81 No)
LAID FIRST BEFORE RIBS
(TO E.S.C.C. SETTING OUT PEGS.)

BRICK ON EDGE RIBS

DIAGRAMMATIC VIEW AT CORNER

GRAVEL
ETC.

BRICK TILE
CORNER

• REVISED 23/12/80
FILLING FOR SQUARES ALTER

PLAN 'A' TYPICAL CORNER

OF BRICKWORK   1:5

Once the chessboard had been made, the metal-framed pieces could be put in position over the green or gold yew plants which are to produce the final, full-size versions. The photographs here give a fine overall view of the chess garden in its setting at Brickwall, where the frames have been protectively painted white or black according to their side in the chess 'game'. Within them, the dark green yews can be seen more prominently inside the black frames than the opposing gold plants in the white frames. In the background can be seen the old yews, now clipped and controlled, that marked the structure of the original garden while, further back, the Elizabethan house itself can be seen beyond a wall that contains the garden with its conical yew walk close to the house.

On pages 90-93 illustrations of the chess pieces reveal the detail of the finished frames and the size of the initial plants. The garden has been meticulously laid out and within a few years will present a fine example of forward planning. Not everyone, of course, will want or be able to place a chess topiary garden within a 60 feet square area in their grounds, but this example has been chosen to show how a formal topiary scheme can be envisaged and brought to fruition by someone wanting to set one out.

The illustrations on this and the opposite page show various views of the chess topiary garden at Brickwall, with the metal-framed black and white pieces set on their gravel squares. In the background the house and original topiary garden trees.

White rook and pawn frames planted with gold yews.

White bishop frame.

Knight with pawns in the background.

Detail of construction of knight showing riveted joints.

90

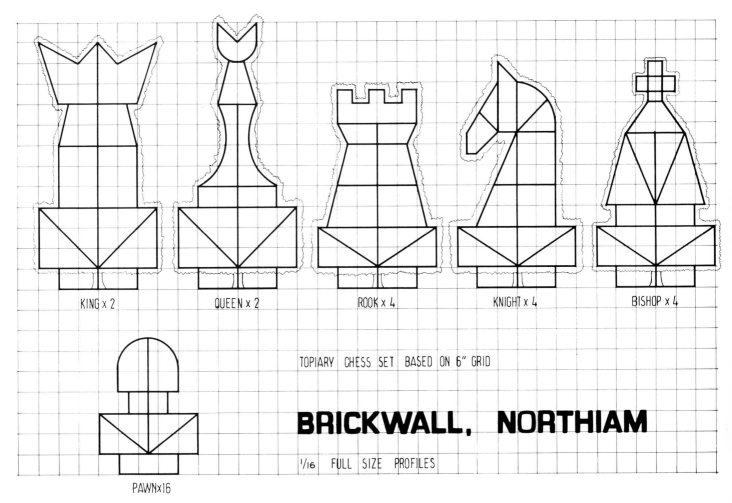

KING x 2   QUEEN x 2   ROOK x 4   KNIGHT x 4   BISHOP x 4

PAWN x 16

TOPIARY CHESS SET BASED ON 6" GRID

BRICKWALL, NORTHIAM

1/16 FULL SIZE PROFILES

Elevations drawn to scale of metal chess piece frames, giving overall outlines and constructional members.

In this case, the black and white squares of the chessboard and the colouring of the chess pieces are in harmony with the black and white timbering of the house. Other colours can be envisaged if a house is of different construction. An amazing sidelight for the chess connoisseur is that the game has reached one move before checkmate — visitors have not yet been asked to specify the move!

After laying down the board, there came the construction, positioning and planting of the chess pieces. These were to be ultimately of green and gold yew, representing black and white chessmen, with the shaping controlled by steel frames designed and built to William Mount's specification. The drawing, above, shows the outlines of the shapes to scale, while the photographs, left, show various pieces with the yews planted within the frames.

The use of frames to control shape and size is a practice dealt with in other parts of this book; it has been developed to a high degree in the United States, and it can be seen from the Brickwall example that frames do help the planner to fix the scale and extent of the topiary well in advance of growth. This is of great assistance where plants do not already exist and where it is very hard to foresee the eventual interrelationship of different future shapes to one another, quite apart from the control of plant structure as the tree grows. In any garden where a series of topiary shapes is being planned, and where they have a formal relationship which is not simply symmetrical, the use of frames of the Brickwall type can be invaluable.

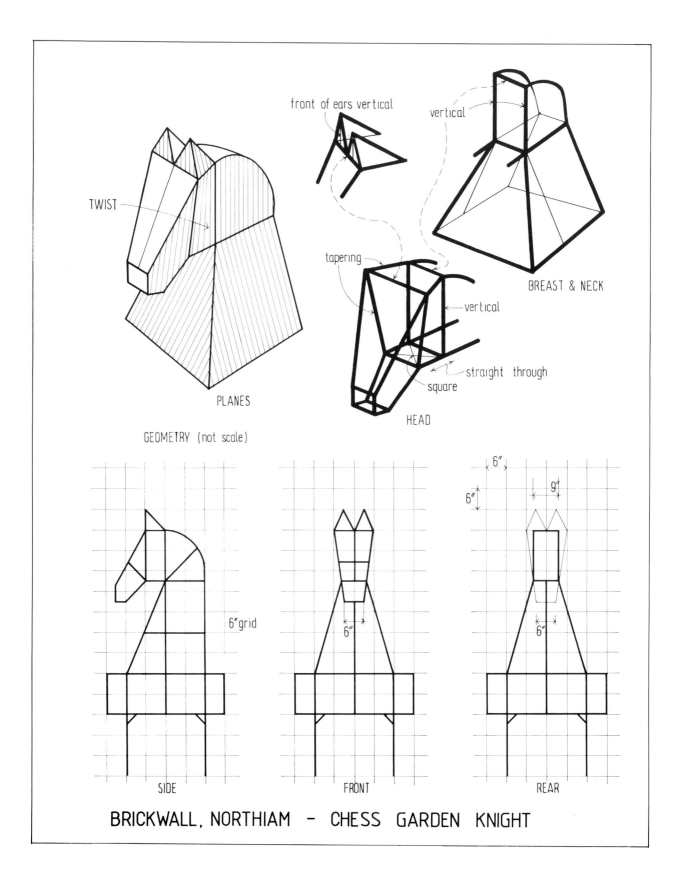

front of ears vertical

vertical

TWIST

vertical

tapering

BREAST & NECK

vertical

straight through

square

PLANES

HEAD

GEOMETRY (not scale)

6″grid

6″

6″

9″

6″

6″

6″

SIDE

FRONT

REAR

BRICKWALL, NORTHIAM – CHESS GARDEN KNIGHT

Knight frame detailed constructionally and showing the work involved for the blacksmith and the thought given to the making of the chess set.

The photograph above shows a knight — which required more complex construction than the other pieces — in position with a recently-planted yew within. The two men give an idea of the size and scale of the project. Below left, the rook frame with golden yew planted. As the yew plants grow they will be clipped to the shape the frame dictates and the frames themselves will become less prominent until, eventually, they will hardly be evident. Below, right, detail of white bishop's frame.

Three other chess sets

On this page a romantic garden in Huntingdon with the yew chess set among old roses and flowers.

Above and right the well-clipped box of the chess set at Little Haseley, Oxfordshire. Below, the Hever chess men in yew.

The house and garden in Hampshire at the beginning of this century. The domed archway has subsequently been removed.

Free-shaping topiary

A garden in Hampshire

The second example of a garden in which topiary plays an important role concerns a charming country farmhouse garden containing topiary formed by free-shaping to the owner's ideas. The garden has formal and informal areas which are used as models for anyone wanting to create this kind of modest, country topiary garden or parts of it. Each section or element of the formal design can be used individually and does not have to be part of an overall layout as shown in the total plan; the three major segments — sundial area, pond garden and parterre — are each quite distinct. They have been combined most happily so that the overall plan, with its major axes at right angles, is excellent, but each gardener will be able to judge for him or herself how these three separate elements, or only one or two of them, could be used for the land available for the purpose.

From the plan of the house and garden, it can be seen that the house is at the lower centre part of the layout. The total area of the grounds has been left out of the plan for simplicity, but there are wilder, natural areas of orchard and grass not shown here. Leading straight from a porch at the front of the house is a path leading to a stone sundial which was in position in 1919. This part of the garden consists of a straight brick path set in grass leading to the sundial, with formal rectangular beds of herbaceous flowers on either side. Another path, of grass, cuts the plan at right angles and leads (to the right) to the pond garden through a charming formal 'gateway' opening in the square yew hedges which enclose the pond. Since the sundial garden does not involve topiary, except for one or two birds close to the house which are shown in the illustrations, it does not require further detailed elaboration. It is, however, enclosed by yew hedges which add to its sense of formality and direction.

The modern version of the bird shown opposite.

96

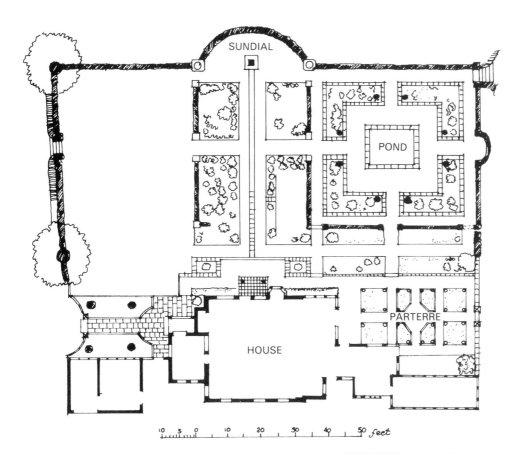

Plan of the house and garden in Hampshire. Only the enclosed, more formal part of the land is shown; orchards and a wild garden have been omitted for the sake of clarity. The house is in the lower centre section of the plan with the formal gardens on two axes, at right angles, leading from it. The strong dark lines show the yew hedges which enclose parts of the garden.

The pond garden is about 50 feet square. Note how the entrances have been arranged to suit the overall garden layout and are not symmetrical whilst at the same time appearing to give symmetry to the arrangement. The paths here are all carefully-mown grass, but could be of brick in the herringbone pattern so much associated with early 'Dutch' gardens. The pairs of box birds flanking each entrance path add charm and formality to the scheme.

The parterre in the lower right section of the plan shows how flower beds arranged in a close grid-like structure can be given a spacious look by chamfering the corners of the four middle beds. This is an extremely simple but effective parterre design which is easy to lay out and control.

The Hampshire garden in the early 1900s, showing the topiary bird which has now altered greatly.

Above, the pond garden showing the formal balls and obelisks developed out of the enclosing yew hedges. Below left, a pair of box birds, and right, a strong abstract bird shape in well-clipped box.

The pond garden is one which we have taken as an element in its own right. It is a fine example of an enclosed garden about 50 feet square, the central feature of which is the square pond. One of the delights of the layout is the way in which the entrances to the area are apparently symmetrical and yet are not so; examination of the plan, shown on page 97, reveals that there are three entrances on one side, two on another, one on another and none in the boundary hedge. The photograph above shows how the entrances, which can be simple openings to start with, have been developed over the years with ball finials and obelisks taking a prominent flanking position. The ball finials have now been slightly

Parterre, showing the brick paving and flowers within tightly-clipped low box hedges. A very simple and effective way to deal with a rectangular area leading to a more open space beyond.

Yew tree in the informal area shown before clipping, with sheeting laid out to catch the clippings. The owner makes the point that it is not so much the clipping that involves so much work, but the clearing up afterwards. Here is a solution to the problem.

altered to an onion shape as a further fancy of the owner — an advantage of the free-shaping method.

The third element in this harmonious Hampshire garden is the parterre, which leads the eye to a pavilion across a lawned area not shown in the plan. The parterre is of formally-patterned box with brick-paved paths leading away from the house. It occupies an area about 40 feet long by 25 feet wide and consists, in essence, of pairs of rectangular beds with clipped box borders set in a formal grid. At the centre, the beds have had their corners chamfered to give a central area and an impression of space. This is a very simple and yet very delightful parterre design which can be made to enclose beds of roses, as shown here, or another formally-controlled plant such as lavender if required.

The garden does not, of course, begin and end with these formal areas, as we have pointed out. There is much more to it than the delightful control of the hedges and the topiary. One of the most pleasant aspects is the way in which the formality reaches out and joins into the naturalistic as the two photographs of a yew tree — before and after clipping — show. The area is a natural one but the yew has suddenly turned formal in the midst of it, providing a contrast which enhances both aspects. This garden is indeed a model for any aspirant topiarist to look at and to learn from. It shows that any garden, however modest, can benefit from imaginative handling of ideas.

The same tree shown after clipping. Its formal shape, pompously dignified among the natural forms of this part of the garden, provides a contrast that enhances both aspects.

Chapter Seven
SOME ENGLISH TOPIARY GARDENS

The creation of the formal garden goes back in influence to the Romans and, hence, its spread across Western Europe to Britain can be charted without difficulty. The revival of such formal gardening and its use of symmetry belongs to the Italian Renaissance and to the great French gardens of the time of Versailles. All these models have been used in Britain, America and further afield; most modern garden architects who belong to a more formal school than that of 'Capability' Brown and the naturalistic landscape gardeners will admit their debt to these earlier models.

The formal gardens which are in existence in England today are either survivors which have been preserved from earlier times, including restorations and the nineteenth century mini-revival of such types, or ones which have been carefully created in recent years when a less labour-intense design is necessary. England is fortunate in possessing some outstandingly well-preserved early topiary gardens and in having some recent creations which show that topiary does not have to be laid down only for future generations. Brickwall and the garden in Hampshire, discussed in the previous chapter, surely demonstrate this fact.

It is at Levens Hall in Cumbria, celebrated in England as one of the earliest surviving topiary gardens, in which Beaumont's designs remain untouched — they have been maintained since they were first carried out in 1690. Beaumont, as we have mentioned earlier, was a pupil of Le Nôtre, who laid out Versailles,

Three topiary specimens at Levens Hall.

Formal topiary in Our Lady's Garden at Levens Hall, Cumbria. This photograph of the most celebrated and one of the earliest topiary gardens in England was taken c.1926.

Athelhampton, Dorset as it was c.1900 when the famous pyramidal yews had just been planted.

and the list of Beaumont's clients in England is both impressive and comprehensive. Levens, however, is the only garden which survives, except for vestiges at Forde Abbey in Dorset. Indeed, the present owner of Levens, Mr. Robin Bagot, had to beat off a Ministry of Transport scheme to put a motorway link road through the focal point of the end of the park in 1970, so the peril to such gardens has not always been in the unenlightened past. The plan of Levens shown in Chapter 1 faithfully follows that of Beaumont, as recorded by Skyring in 1730. The extraordinary shapes, like abstract sculpture, remain in the imagination long after they have been seen.

Abstract shapes were not the hallmark of most early gardens. A rigid formality characterises many of them, as the pyramidal yews at Brickwall confirm. The remarkable pyramid yew garden at Athelhampton in Dorset, with its Great Terrace flanked by two garden houses, designed by Francis Inigo Thomas, brings France immediately to mind despite the fact that Athelhampton has a remarkable history which goes well back to before the Norman Conquest. The splendid yews of this garden, each over 25 feet tall, which are set out around the sunken lawn with its formal fish pond and fountain, are strikingly sharp and superbly maintained. They are not all of the same species and the acute observer can appreciate the subtle differences in yew textures from pyramid to pyramid.

Detail of some of Great Dixter's famous topiary.

101

Above left, a pair of 'French chocolate pots' at Great Dixter. Above right, top, the Knightshayes hunt — hounds racing along the top of the hedge, and below, detail of one of the hounds.

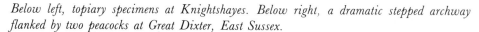

Below left, topiary specimens at Knightshayes. Below right, a dramatic stepped archway flanked by two peacocks at Great Dixter, East Sussex.

Chilham Castle, Kent.

Above, Godington Park; below, Athelhampton.

Above, Levens Hall; below, Lytes Carey.

These birds at Great Dixter guard the entrance to the old barn. A fine example of a well-balanced design.

If it was the Romans who first brought topiary to England there could be no more appropriate site for it than Chilham Castle in Kent. It is said that the first skirmish between the recently-landed troops of Julius Caesar and the Britons took place in sight of the hill on which Chilham now stands. Among the dead on that occasion was a tribune, Quintus Laberius Durus, who lies buried on Juliberry Down, on the opposite side of the river from Chilham Castle. Many Roman remains have been found at Chilham, including those of a senate house, but its rich history from Saxon to Norman times onwards is less relevant to this book than the laying out of its gardens by John Tradescant in the early seventeenth century. Tradescant is one of the most famous gardeners of his period — he was appointed Royal Gardener in 1629 — and at Chilham he constructed a large walled garden laid out in a series of terraces with gazebos at the eastern end. When Sir Dudley Digges, the builder of the Jacobean house at Chilham, went on a diplomatic mission to Russia, Tradescant accompanied him and brought back many plants, including the first larches to be brought to the country. The formal gardens which remain at Chilham owe much to Tradescant's design even if they have been subsequently altered and expanded. In the eighteenth century 'Capability' Brown worked on the Chilham gardens and produced his now famous far-reaching landscape effects, so that most of the formal gardens were swept aside and it is fortunate that the terraces, walls and lawns still remain.

As an example of something less grand than Chilham, Athelhampton and Levens, the quiet mellow age of the old manor house at Lytes Cary, in Somerset, set in farming country, provides a soothing contrast. From the thirteenth century to the eighteenth century it was owned by the Lyte family which produced a botanist squire, John Lyte. He, in 1578, dedicated his 'Lyte's Herbal' to Queen Elizabeth 'from my poore house at Lytescarie'. By the early twentieth century the house was in a regrettably ruined state and, with the gardens, was restored by Sir Walter Jenner, who left it to the National Trust. It is a charming example of a medieval manor house and although nothing remains of the botanic garden laid out by John Lyte, the present garden gives an impression of quiet permanence, with a solid march of rounded 'cottage-loaf' yews leading to a distant dovecot, and large moulded cylinders of box ranked along the stone walls flanking the garden.

At Godington Park, near Ashford in Kent, the work of Sir Reginald Blomfield, a pupil of Richard Norman Shaw, can be seen in the formal gardens laid out in the late 1890s beside a house dating back to medieval times. Godington is a typical English house in the sense that it has been altered or added to in every century since the seventeenth, taking advantage of those happy days before planning authorities could slap listing restrictions on domestic buildings to prevent their owners from doing what they liked with them. In Blomfield's formal designs the charm of the house and its Renaissance gables are echoed in the shaping of the yew hedges. A formally-enclosed area with statuary is defined by yew hedges with pyramidally-shaped obelisks of yew at each corner and, further away, layered topiary specimens in yew provide sculptural effects.

A yew peacock at Great Dixter.

A view of the formal topiary on the topiary lawn at Great Dixter.

At Knightshayes, near Tiverton, Devon, the topiary and house are the creation of the same period — the 1870s — even though the present owners have modified and extended the gardens to make them a justly celebrated attraction. Knightshayes was designed by William Burges, the famous architect of the High Gothic School, who built it for J. Heathcote Amory, Liberal M.P. for Tiverton, whose father-in-law had moved his lace-making business to the town from Leicestershire because of the Luddite riots. It is a robust, two-coloured stone house in what is known as the 'muscular' Gothic style. The views across the Exe valley from the house are superb and the balance of control in the garden, which is an extensive one of twenty-five acres, has been very well handled indeed. The topiary section is confined to the terraces near the house and includes massive yew hedges which enclose a secluded pool with a statue, stone benches and a weeping pear tree, seen in the section on hedges in Chapter 3. At Knightshayes there is a charming fox hunt along the top of one of the terrace hedges and this is illustrated on page 102.

The restoration of Great Dixter in Sussex by the topiary specialist and author, Nathaniel Lloyd, who bought the property in 1910, has created a fine topiary legacy which is currently maintained by his son, Christopher Lloyd, also a well known garden authority and writer. The house was restored and extended by Sir Edwin Lutyens before the First World War so that now, inside impressive formal yew hedges with battlemented arched 'doorways', the various sections of the garden are sheltered and laid out. Topiary specimens, including those adorning a special topiary lawn, include peacocks on formal, pyramidal yew bases, formal conical layered shapes and a pair of spectacular sculptured birds with high, arched tails. The specimens outside the topiary lawn add solemn formality to the profuse flower beds of the other sections of the garden and the differing levels of the site enable fascinating perspectives to be obtained.

More yew topiary at Great Dixter.

The white garden at Hidcote with simple box topiary in the 'cottage garden' tradition. It is enclosed by yew hedges.

A detail of the above illustration, showing the plump birds sitting on their pedestals.

No chapter on the role of formal topiary hedges in England would be complete, when arriving at the twentieth century, without mentioning one of its great stars: the garden at Hidcote. Brief details of Sir Walter Jenner's restoration of Lytes Cary in this century have already been mentioned. Chapter 6 describes two modern English topiary gardens in detail. This chapter is to end, as perhaps it should, with a mention of Hidcote, in Gloucestershire. Its owner and creator, Lawrence Johnston, was born of American parents in Paris where he was brought up until he went to Trinity College, Cambridge. He subsequently became a British citizen and served in the Boer War, returning as a major. In about 1907 he received the windy farm and 280 acres at Hidcote as a gift from his mother and took ten acres out of the fields to create a garden, assisted by Norah Lindsay. Eventually the garden became the property of the National Trust, the first property ever to be acquired by the Trust solely for its garden. There is not sufficient space to describe Hidcote adequately here, but the hedges of many kinds and, indeed, of mixtures such as box and yew together, are an outstanding feature of the garden. They were, of course, necessary for protection against the wind, but the design of the garden also allows them to create numerous separate sub-gardens or rooms, each of different character to the next. Hidcote is not a garden that could be created, now, by anyone other than those possessed of enormous resources, but it is an inspiration to many of lesser disposable opportunities. Its carefully-designed hedges remind us that this sort of framework is one that does not take more than a lifetime to create. The formal structure needed for a garden, whether it be of yew, box, holly, beech or privet, can be laid down now and enjoyed within a reasonable number of years from its planting.

Part of the pillar garden at Hidcote. These yew pillars surround a simple lawn; at the base they are planted with flowers which act as a foil to their severity.

A pair of topiary peacocks in yew at Hidcote at the entrance to the pool garden; this is surrounded by architectural yew hedging.

Chapter Eight
CONTEMPORARY DUTCH TOPIARY

Young spirals in the process of being shaped.

In the history of topiary briefly outlined in Chapter 1 it was pointed out that in the thirteenth century the Dutch laid out their gardens with mathematical precision due to the shortage of land available. When the English came to set out formal gardens in the Golden Age of the sixteenth century, such gardens were referred to as 'Dutch' even though they were also based on French and Italian models. This nomenclature was particularly reinforced in the seventeenth century when William of Orange arrived in England bringing a taste for clipped yews with him. The topiary tradition is, therefore, of very long standing in Holland and, even in 1904, when Curtis and Gibson published their *Book of Topiary,* it is quite clear that Holland was a major source of supply, inspiration and technical knowledge for English nurseymen and gardeners.

Aalsmeer and the Boskoop area, near Gouda, were particularly concentrated sources of specialised topiary grown to meet an enormous demand. Nurseries could afford to take a long-term view of their businesses and provided examples in yew as well as the more plentiful box for export to England and America. However, with the increased cost of nursery production, changes in fashion, and the nature of modern garden demand, a rapid decline has taken place both in the number of nurseries willing to supply topiary and in the type available — nearly all modern Dutch topiary from nursery supplies is box of the *Buxus sempervirens* variety. The remaining growers in the Boskoop area have happily reported a very recent upsurge in interest and signs of a resurgence in demand for their work, perhaps due to the influence of the popularity of the formal town garden. This type of topiary is, however, a small, specialised branch of the Dutch nursery industry which merits detailed attention as such.

The grower of box topiary must calculate on at least six years of growth from the preliminary tiny plants before a suitable shape can be formed into a recognisably commercial and saleable form. Dutch box topiary is of a smaller scale and different proportion to the larger types found in English and American gardens where yew and privet are often shaped after many years of growth. This is not to say that modern Dutch topiary is not still much exported to England, but it is generally intended for use in pots and containers where the scale is quite different from that of the country garden. Topiary of this kind is most frequently found close to the house or building it accompanies and is not much seen in distant view. Its charm lies in its diminutive dimensions, which are easily adapted to smaller spaces.

Apart from formal topiary involving cones, pyramids, spirals and balls, the Dutch are fond of animal shapes which appeal to children, such as squirrels, peacocks and, particularly, teddy bears. Other fantasies include jugs, flowers baskets, human forms, ships, crowns, anchors and even, perhaps predictably, windmills. It is quite an experience to contemplate a field of box teddy bears marching solemnly beside a placid canal, but if you are in Boskoop such a vision can meet the eyes which, turning away, may encounter grave ranks of green-leaved peacocks heading in another direction!

A Dutch peacock amid other plants at Wisley.

Topiary on lawn outside the Horticultural Museum in Boskoop.

Box seedlings are planted fairly close together and separated further as they develop. Leader shoots are retained for vertical shapes such as cones and pyramids, whilst spreading side shoots can be adapted for peacocks and similar birds. Variegated box is considered to be too brittle for topiary work of this kind and the more supple *Buxus sempervirens* is more suitable for adaption to wire stiffening and framing. As the plants grow and develop the final shape to which they will be put becomes more evident and, in addition to wire stiffening, judicious pruning is carried out in the spring after any danger of frost is safely past.

The three illustrations of contemporary Dutch topiary show, from left to right:

Box squirrel, grown from a bushy plant with multiple stems rather than a leader shoot. The body is produced by grouping half of the stems round a vertical stake while the tail is made by grouping the other half round a stake set at an angle. The directions for the production of a peacock detailed overleaf set out the principles for growing this kind of topiary, which takes about eight years to develop.

A squirrel in course of formation, clearly showing how the form is achieved.

A typical Dutch peacock produced in the Boskoop area of Holland, where this particular type of topiary has been a speciality of the growers in the area for many years. The method required to produce it from a 2 foot high, four year old plant is described in detail on the following pages.

To produce a peacock in box *(Buxus sempervirens)*
from an approx. 24in. high plant:

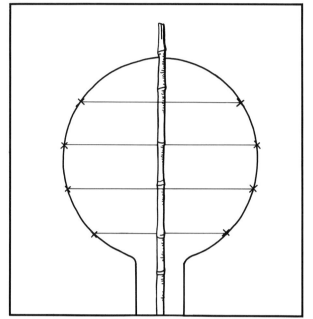

This peacock was made following the method described on these pages.

1. Make a frame from galvanised wire, bending it into a hoop shape as shown but taking care that the two ends are straight because they will be pushed into the soil to help anchor the frame. Attach four horizontal pieces of galvanised wire to the frame at equal spaces as shown, either by tying them to the hoop with wire or by soldering them. Finally, take a piece of bamboo taller than the hoop and thread it between the horizontal wires as shown. This will eventually be driven into the soil to anchor the hoop-shaped frame.

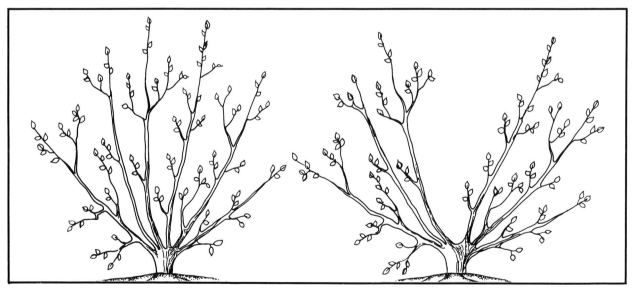

2. The box bush illustrated is diagrammatical and is deliberately drawn rather sparse-looking to help illustrate the method. In reality, the box bush used would be much bushier and leafier. This multi-stemmed type is the best to use for a peacock, rather than the more vertical, single-stemmed type used for cones and spheres.

3. Separate the multi-stemmed bush approximately in half in a vertical plane. About three stems to each side are needed as a minimum. For convenience whilst working one set can be loosely tied together to keep the stems out of the way while the other set is being worked on.

4. *Insert the hooped frame and bamboo vertically in the ground behind one set of stems. Remember to push both the bamboo stake and galvanised wire ends firmly into the ground to anchor the frame. Spread the stems evenly in a 'fan' across the hooped frame and tie them with twist stems or garden twine to the frame. Do not tie the stems too tightly as this will constrict their growth.*

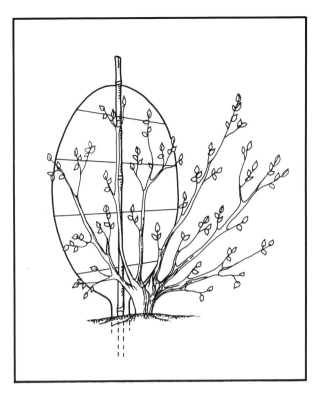

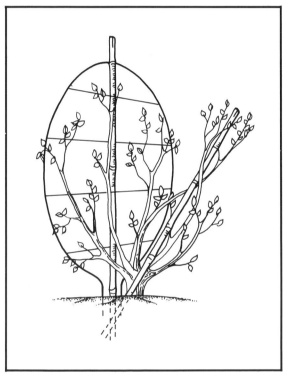

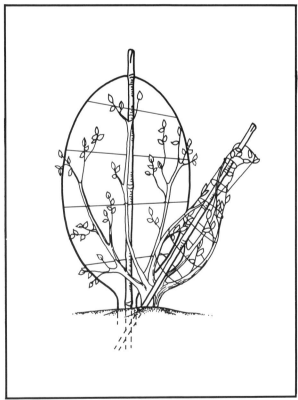

5. *With the tail secured, push another bamboo stake into the ground at 30 degrees to the vertical, close to the first bamboo stake. Make sure that it is deeply and firmly fixed in position. This will give you the angle of the body and head. Take the longest of the three (or more) remaining shoots and tie it loosely to the bamboo. This will eventually form the head and neck. The remaining stems are needed to form the body thickness of the peacock at the base, so they are woven round the angled bamboo, crossing over each other to give bulk. Always weave spare shoots and stems into this section; do not cut off spare shoots. Tie the woven stems loosely to secure them in position.*

6. *A final view of the completed peacock with the loose ties visible on the body. The beak can be formed by pulling down a small shoot and tying it with thin wire or twine to the top tie. The bush can be trimmed with scissors as it growns into shape. This type of topiary is ideal for tubs for terraces or patios.*

Sold — peacock with roots carefully encased in sacking awaiting pick-up by delivery van.

Advertisement poster from a Dutch topiary nursery in Aalsmeer showing the wide variety of shapes which were once offered to the public by these growers. The industry has reduced in size now but some of these shapes are still the speciality of Boskoop growers.

To form this bowl use a plant which has at least six stems growing from the base. Place a wire hanging basket frame in the middle of the stems. Secure the frame to the base and carefully fan out the stems around the outside of the basket and tie them to the metal. Eventually the plant will grow in and hide the frame. Turn regularly if plant is in a container.

112

A field of teddy bears beside a Dutch canal, providing an infant's delight in the midst of the sober industry so typical of Holland.

Charming typical Dutch group of teddy bear, spiral, and Berlin stem, all very popular forms from the Boskoop area.

Above, basket formed in the same way as the bowl, opposite, but with a handle. Right, top and bottom, a typical selection of Dutch topiary. Far right, topiary cones at least six years old and 2-3 feet high.

*How formal topiary —
mostly in yew — is used
to decorate some American
gardens.*

Chapter Nine
AMERICAN TOPIARY

Generally speaking, the development of topiary in the United States of America has followed three broad streams:

1. Garden topiary of the type already described in a European context, both in grand formal gardens and, very frequently, in the small number of formal clipped plants seen in many front gardens.

2. Wire- and metal-framed topiary of the kind already described in Chapter 4 and shown at Brickwall in Chapter 6, but with much more development of widely available ready-made forms.

3. Indoor and outdoor pre-formed topiary, in which frames are filled with sphagnum moss, and then ivy or similar creepers and flowers are planted into this 'dummy' to give the desired external effect. This, in turn, has led to combinations such as the creations at Disneyland, where a combination of the techniques of wire-frame and pre-formed topiary are used. This pre-formed topiary is described in Chapter 10.

1. Garden topiary

The European visitor to the United States will nearly always be struck by the almost severe formality of the traditional American residential front garden. The house sits in a mown grass area without flower beds, but usually adorned by trees or evergreen shrubs or bushes. Very often there will be a group of three or more small clipped yew bushes or similar evergreens set in the front lawn or perhaps close to the house on either side of the front door. These are often the only softening link between the house and the garden. Three such gardens are illustrated here to show how this habit is accepted as a traditional way of decorating the front of the house.

Apart from this widespread taste, the United States abounds in many fine examples of formal topiary gardens, from the New England style, close to that of Europe, to tropical and sub-tropical variations on the West Coast and elsewhere. A great deal of careful research and painstaking development has been carried out in the U.S.A. into the nature of the plants suitable for topiary and the best methods of obtaining successful shaped specimens. Only a few examples can be given here because the richness and variety of American garden topiary, both formal and whimsical, prohibits comprehensive coverage due to the sheer space that would be necessary.

Topiary gardens at Longwood, showing the formal yew shapes beyond the lions guarding the entrance.

Above, another section of the topiary garden at Longwood, Pennsylvania. Right, an old photograph of a garden in Maryland designed by Harold Peto.

A selection of privet animals at Green Animals, Rhode Island.

New formal box circular hedges will be developed from fresh, replacement planting round one of the principal privet animals at Green Animals, Rhode Island.

Lyre bird topiary and formal classical shapes at Ladew, Maryland.

Green Animals, Rhode Island

An exceptional garden whose stylised privet hedging has already been illustrated in Chapter 3 is Green Animals, an unusual and charming garden of seven acres at Narragansett Bay, Portsmouth, near Newport. The house and land were bought in 1872 by Thomas Brayton who, with his Portuguese gardener Joseph Carreiro, undertook this fascinating arrangement of hedges, animals and human shapes. Appropriately enough, Brayton's daughter Alice continued to maintain and develop the grounds altogether with her gardener, who was Carreiro's son-in-law, George Mendorca. In 1974 the property was left to the Newport Preservation Society and opened to the public, with the result that there has been considerable preservation and restoration of the plants.

At present the garden consists of about eighty topiary pieces. Approximately half are of American boxwood and golden boxwood. Animals such as the camel, giraffe, elephant and bear, together with the peacocks, are sculptured from Californian privet. Geometrical and formal designs are of boxwood. Although the giraffe originally had a very long neck, this was damaged by a hurricane in 1954, so that the length of this splendid feature is, alas, somewhat curtailed now. Alice Brayton was particularly fond of the whimsical aspects of topiary and the policeman, ostrich, and rooster are at the heart of her own area, known as Miss Alice's Garden.

Ladew Gardens, Jarretsville, Moncton, Maryland

This fine topiary garden, about fifteen miles north of Baltimore, was started when Mr. Ladew bought the house and land in 1931. The garden was then non-existent apart from a couple of maple trees. Mr. Ladew spent a considerable amount of his time in England, where he was a keen foxhunter. On one occasion, whilst out with the hounds in Beaufort country, he saw a yew hedge with a topiary foxhunt in full cry along the top, rather like that of Knightshayes illustrated on page 102. When he enquired as to the owner he found that it was indeed the Duke of Beaufort's cousin, Lady Sophie Scott, who explained the technique to him. She used frames which she had made for her locally and she grew the yew into and around them. After the frames were filled she kept the shapes smartly clipped. This inspired Mr. Ladew and to this day the visitor can see the result, not only in the splendid hunt chasing across the green grass, pursued by a rider who is jumping the hedge, but also in the many other aspects of the gardens.

At the entrance to Ladew is a pretty garden cottage and close to it is a big yew tree clipped into four tiers surmounted by a rooster. This specimen was brought to the site by Mr. Ladew when he moved from Long Island proving, like Longwood, that topiary can be transplanted if sufficient care is given to the task. Numerous different gardens are to be found when the visitor penetrates the grounds, including hybrid rhododendrons, a berry garden, spring garden, lilies,

The formal pyramidal topiary garden at Ladew.

A charming view of the French hen at Ladew, sitting on a nest which forms the base. Formal pyramidal topiary can be seen in the background.

azaleas, roses and peonies, not to mention such features as the ticket office from the Old Tivoli Theatre, but the topiary enthusiast will pass these for the first topiary garden, found close to the house. In this the specimens are all of yew, straight *Taxus cuspidata,* whereas the hedges are of hemlock (*Tsuga canadensis*). Clipping of the celebrated specimens, which include the lyre birds, sea horses and many more, goes on all year round here rather than being confined to a particular season.

To go down to the great bowl area, the visitor passes the long line of topiary swans riding the hedge waves and then passes pyramids up the steps to a pair of French hens on hemlock rests to a wonderful garlanded and windowed hedge on the top terrace. Through these extraordinary windows in the hedge, which is redolent of the most elaborate creations of the eighteenth century in Europe, are views of the countryside beyond. All the tall hedges are of hemlock (*Tsuga canadensis*). Other delights at Ladew include a Chinese junk furnished with 'real' red sails, a full-size giraffe and a Buddha on the hill. In short, Ladew is a creation to rival a topiary fantasy in any part of the globe and reflects its founder's enthusiasm to this day.

Longwood Gardens, Kennet Square, Pennsylvania

The history of Longwood Gardens goes back to the year 1700, when a Quaker family called Pierce acquired the land from William Penn. The Pierces planted trees and created one of America's finest tree parks, which was preserved when Pierre S. du Pont (1870-1954) bought the property and became the primary designer of Longwood Gardens.

The gardens now have many different areas, including the trees, a peony

Photos on this page by Dick Keen, Longwood Gardens.

These splendid formal specimens at Longwood, Pennsylvania, show the versatility of the yew tree.

garden and a water garden quite apart from the roses, but the topiary gardens outdoors were started in 1936, when yews were planted as formal settings for the Amalemic sundial. Eleven large mounds, four cones and a horseshoe hedge were put in, the horseshoe hedge forming the backdrop. The subsequent development of the topiary garden is an interesting example of how topiary can be moved from its original location to another, depending of course on the skill of those involved in arranging such a delicate task. The additions to the Longwood topiary, obtained from elsewhere, were chronologically as follows:

1958: Thirty separate figures were bought from Bismark Estate, in Bayville, Long Island, together with some hedges.

1963: Eight figures were added, having been acquired from the Charles Fiore Nursery in Prairie View, Illinois.

1971: Two urns were added from the Taylor Arboretum, Chester, Pa.

1980: Five figures were added from the Longwood Nursery itself.

The garden now has a total of sixty-one pieces, which include birds, dog, chair, table, rabbit and similar creations, apart from formal shapes such as spirals and cones. The plants in this garden are all trained and maintained without the use of frames or wire. To keep the shapes, much of the shearing and clipping is done by electric shears or hedge trimmers and mechanical hoisting devices are used instead of ladders and scaffolding to minimise the work necessary to gain access to the upper areas where maintenance is needed.

At Longwood the plants are all yews. *Taxus cuspidata* (*capitata*) is used for the mounded forms and upright forms. Some horizontal shapes are in *Taxus xmedia densiformus*.

This small selection of gardens is perhaps more representative of the Eastern style of topiary, which is closer to its European counterparts than the sub-tropical and tropical styles found elsewhere in the U.S.A., particularly California, where the natural roundness of certain species is used to great effect in formal garden arrangements. The amount and scale of topiary in the U.S.A. is very encouraging in view of the fact that so much of it is modern, of recent conception, and often quite unique in design.

One of a pair of decorative shapes which flank the bottom of a stairway at Longwood Gardens.

119

2. Wire- or metal-framed topiary

In the U.S.A. wire-frame topiary for outside use in gardens follows almost exactly the same pattern as that in Europe and the frames are used, as at Brickwall in Chapter 6, to give guidance on the future shaping of the plants and to provide an idea of the future relationship of the topiary within its overall plan. This idea is difficult to visualise without the frames and the reader is referred to the description of Brickwall to get a detailed case-history of this concept. It is a fascinating speculation, when looking at the wire frames for the fox and hounds at Knightshayes in Chapter 4, to draw a sequence leading from Mr. Ladew's vision of Lady Sophie Scott's wire hounds in the Beaufort hunt country to Ladew in Maryland and back to Devon again, where the yew and wire chase continues.

Above, an excellent example of a young camel at Ladew, not yet grown into its frame. Right, the structural frame is still visible at the bottom of this formal shaped plant, used to emphasise the garden steps at Ladew.

Above, the fox hunt at the entrance to Ladew gardens, Maryland. A horse and rider pursue the pack by leaping the gate at the side of the lawn.

Below, detail of hound at Ladew, showing a new frame in position, designed to assist reshaping of a plant which had become distorted with age.

Right, the hunt in full cry, with the fox, hopefully, making for cover.

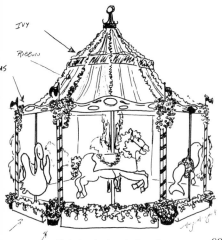

Original sketch for the Longwood Carousel by Mary Mizdail.
Below and on the opposite page, drawings of some of the carousel animals.

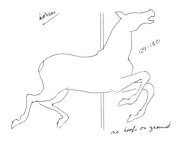

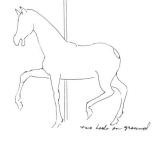

A selection of typical American wire frames used for pre-formed topiary construction.

Chapter Ten
PRE~FORMED TOPIARY

In this section we come to deal with a creative addition to the world of topiary that is almost, but not quite, uniquely American. Certainly the development of this type of topiary work owes its existence and energy to several American centres, not least of which are Longwood Gardens. However, we also illustrate the work of the Torbay Borough Council in this field. Although it can be argued that this form of shaping is not true topiary in the classic tradition, it does have a place today, as it can be made quite easily and in a relatively short time. It can also be kept quite happily indoors, on patios or terraces and even outside, if growing instructions are adhered to. Much research has been done over the last twenty-five years in this field, particularly by Longwood Gardens, which always has magnificent examples on display. The various techniques which are used to achieve these topiaries are explained below in terms of the three main types of this particular genre, which are:

1. A frame filled with soil and moss, with many plants 'plugged' into the frame. Perhaps the most spectacular example of this type is the celebrated Longwood Carousel.
2. A hollow frame filled with moss which has one plant planted into the frame, which has become the container.
3. A single potted plant which has a wire frame anchored to it. The plant is then trained over the frame.

The main hall at Longwood Gardens with huge hanging balls of chrysanthemums which will be in flower for Christmas. Pages 134 and 135 give details of how to make similar balls.

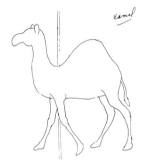

camel

Could be made with two humps if you prefer. Camel would be slightly larger than horses. It may be necessary to make in three sections. Should it have a tail?

back hoofs on ground

goat

In November 1985, Longwood held a Chrysanthemum Festival which featured one of the most spectacular creations to come from this very imaginative garden. This was the carousel shown in the photographs overleaf, and while it is something which every individual would wish to attempt, it contains features which are so striking that they are well worth describing in case an amateur topiarist is keen to try making one of the items.

The carousel illustrations are perhaps the best explanation of this outstanding floral invention but for the sake of enthusiasts, and for the record, the materials used included:

Creeping fig was used on the camel.

Ivies were used on all the other creatures.

Hedera helix 'Calico' covered the goat.

Horses were covered in *Ficus* and *Hedera helix* 'Eva', 'Gertrud Strauss', 'Appaloosa' and 'Telecurl'.

Manes and tails consisted of bright chrysanthemums.

The top of the carousel had flowers and garlands of 'Manda's Crested' ivy.

Because this had been such a successful creation, Longwood kept the exhibit from autumn to the end of the Christmas season. In early December, the tails and manes were replaced by strands of ivy. Eight different cultivars were used, which added texture and subtle colour to the display.

Large topiary framed structures, including animals

To produce pre-formed large topiary examples such as camels, horses and so on, is a lengthy business and requires considerable maintenance. The procedure which is normally followed for these large pieces is as follows:

1. The metal frames are built and put into position.
2. Large frames are fitted with styrofoam cores to reduce the weight of the finished topiary.
3. Sphagnum moss or soil mixture is used as a growing medium, depending on the type of plant covering the animal.
4. The plants used both in Britain and America for covering these large structures include creeping fig, baby's tears, pilea ferns, woolly thyme, sagina, spider plant, succulents, sedum, sempervivum and other varieties listed on pages 138 and 139.

The road-runner — an American bird immortalised in topiary at Longwood Gardens.

123

Left, above and below, horse, goat, lion and camel, all complete and in final position on the carousel.

The horse and camel in course of construction — note the white flower pot in position to take the cascade chrysanthemums used for the tail.

The Longwood Carousel in its final grandeur, together with close-ups of one of the splendid horses, with its mane of bright chrysanthemums, and a dignified reindeer complete with saddle and reins.

Photos on these pages by Dick Keen, Longwood Gardens.

To make a duck using pre-formed frame:

Pre-formed topiary type 1

The Longwood and Torbay topiaries are examples of the type 1 variety. The method used is illustrated by a simpler example on these pages, showing how a duck can be made.

A frame, stuffed with moss and soil, has suitable plants pushed into it at regular intervals on critical points. These plants spread to cover the solid surface and thus give the desired shape. A recommended plant for this is *Ficus pumila,* or creeping fig. The procedure is as follows:

1. Take the frame which, in America, can be a ready-made type purchased from a garden shop or, elsewhere, an individually made one of the desired size. Fix the frame securely to a wooden base. The drawings shown here can be used as a pattern, with suitable scaling-up to achieve the size required.

2. As with a hanging basket, start lining the frame with moist sphagnum moss. Only line a section at a time, as shown in figure 2, so that the plants can be arranged in tiers which emerge from the moss.

3. Fill the moss lining with potting compost and arrange the first layer of plants evenly around the edge. A minimum of four plants should be used, depending on the size of the frame. (N.B. the compost should be soilless, e.g. vermiculite.)

4. Continue to fill the frame by adding another section of moss lining, taking care that no soil is visible around the stems of the first layer of plants. Add potting compost as before and arrange the next layer of plants evenly in the same way as before.

5. Continue the procedure until the whole frame is filled. Try to place plants with long trailers close to the tail and head ends, since these long trailers can be trained up the moss to cover the sections which are difficult to fill with soil. The extremities are normally only filled with moss for this reason. The moss can be tied in position with fishing line if the sections are difficult to arrange.

6. Pin the plant trailers to the filled frame, spreading them evenly to achieve a uniform finish. Hairpins are normally used for this.

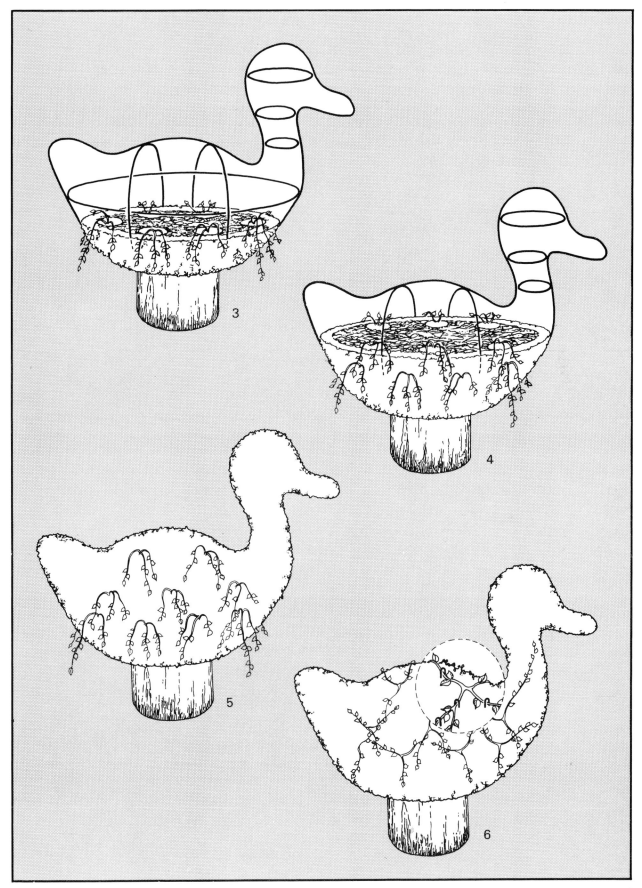

3

4

5

6

These magnificent structures were built by the Borough of Torbay for various Chelsea Flower Shows. After the show they are positioned on the seafront at Torquay and are kept alive outside until the end of October.

A full-size type 'B' London bus, in use in London between 1909 and 1926. It is, to date, the largest exhibit Torbay Borough Council has made.

A charming piece of plant sculpture — the Pied Piper with the rats — shown at the Chelsea Flower Show.

The Torquay topiary at the Chelsea Flower Show

Although pre-formed topiary is perhaps primarily associated with America, there is a well-known exhibition series produced by the Borough of Torbay in Devon, England, which exhibits this type of decorative plant sculpture at the Chelsea Flower Show as well as in its home territory of Torquay. The concept of these three-dimensional sculptures stemmed originally from developing the traditional seaside crest or carpet bedding designs which are to be seen in many boroughs whose proud escutcheons are displayed in plants or flowers. In the case of the Parks and Recreation Services of Torbay, a start was made in 1983 with a thatched cottage with walls and roof fabricated in wood and covered with a welded mesh grille to form a cavity between for planking. From this relatively small structure, technical advances have been made which show improvements year by year. The largest so far has been a vintage London bus of the 1909-1926 era in full size, which is shown above.

The aim is to create a plant sculpture which can survive a six month display period starting in early May and lasting until the end of October. The all steel mesh fabricated structure has to hold sufficient compost and nutrients to last this entire period. Its packed walls are planted at a density of one plant per square inch, adding up to a tremendous figure of 70,000 plants for the bus structure.

Plants used are *Pyrethrum, Alternanthera, Sedum, Echeveria, Herniaria, Sempervirens,* all of which exhibit various leaf colourings such as yellow, gold, red, grey, green, etc. Those which extend in growth during the summer can be trimmed back to the required shape or even shaped further to produce a textured surface of even growth. Watering is most important, at narrow extremities especially, since narrow sections dry out. The peat-based compost is difficult to re-wet when overdried, so that continuous moisture is essential. Almost any shape can be formed but scale drawings must take account of plant growth; sizes must be reduced to allow for growth, otherwise thickening can distort the shape envisaged.

A different sculpture is produced every year and a great deal of creative effort goes into each exhibit. It is perhaps this particular borough which had done most to bring this branch of topiary to the British gardening public, who are always enthusiastic admirers of the exhibits on the Torbay stand.

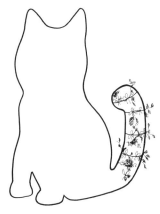

Detail showing tying of tail section.

Table top topiaries

Materials needed for the three types described in this section are:
1. Plants — ivy, ficus etc.
2. Frames — purchased or homemade.
3. Moss (spagnum).
4. Fern pins or hairpins.
5. Potting mix — soilless and lightweight such as peat or vermiculite.
6. Fishing line (cloth type preferable) or string.

Pre-formed topiary type 1

This consists of many plants being plugged into a frame containing moss and growing compost. This type of topiary has been described in detail on pages 126 and 127. Two further examples of this topiary are shown on this page.

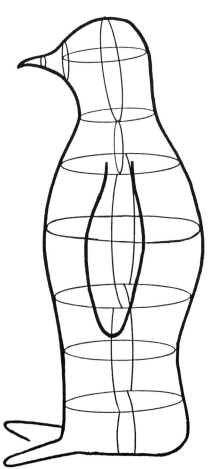

Empty penguin frame.

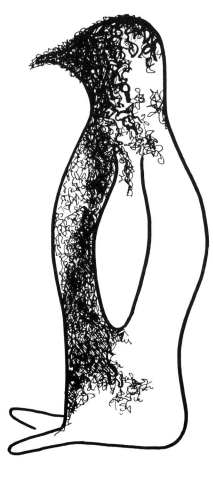

Partially completed penguin.

Completed bird with lighter coloured plants used to 'plug' the chest.

130

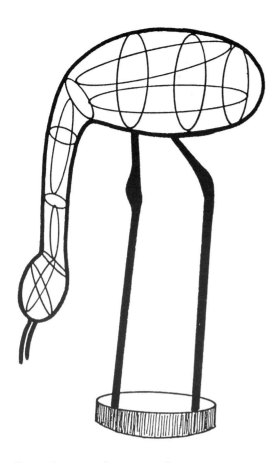

Above: the empty frame secured to a wooden block.

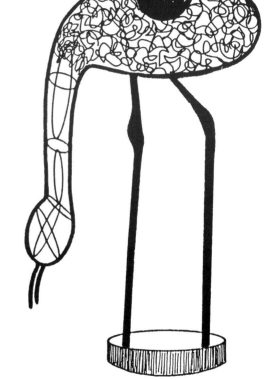

Right: the partially completed bird with a single plant in position on top of the body.

Pre-formed topiary type 2

Single plant in hollow frame filled with moss

1. Use an ivy which has self-branching runners, such as 'Green Feather', a type which has been used successfully.
2. Soak the sphagnum moss until soft.
3. Secure the frame to the base.
4. Fill the frame with moss, in the same way as you would a hanging basket, but leave a central hole big enough to take your plant. Insert the potless plant into the hole and pack moss around the root ball.
5. Cover the top of the root ball thinly with moss.
6. Spread the runners evenly over the frame and pin them into position with small hairpins.

   The ostrich frame here has been planted in this way; eventually the ivy will thicken out and grow over the frame, being caught in position as the plant lengthens.

131

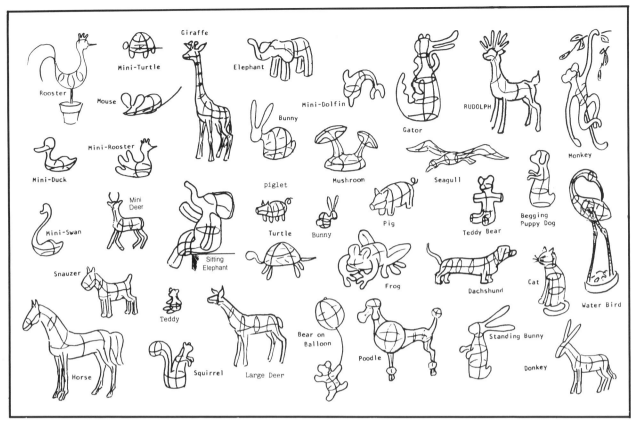

Typical frames for pre-formed topiary.

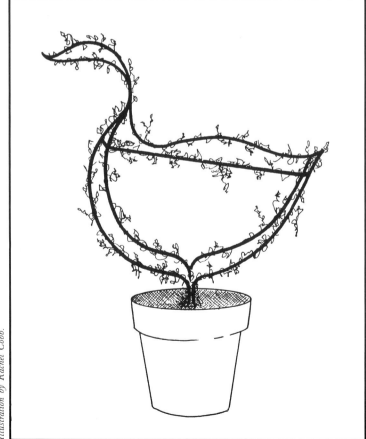

Illustration by Rachel Cobb.

Pre-formed topiary type 3
Single potted plant with frame

1. Assume you have bought a well grown plant in a pot, such as an ivy of the goldheart variety, i.e. one with a good trailing habit.
2. Position your shaped frame securely into the pot.
3. Gently and evenly tie the ivy runner up and over the frame. Use twist ties or string. Make sure not to tie too tightly or the plant will not be able to grow.

Right, a type 1 topiary cat using Hedera helix 'Piroutte' and 'Calico'. Both this and type 3 are produced by Longwood Gardens.

Left, an example of type 3, the plants covering the silhouette shape.

A selection from the many different 'topiaries' produced at Meadowbrook Gardens, U.S.A.

Hanging monkey at Meadowbrook, U.S.A., produced from Ficus pumila, a creeping fig. This is a type 2 topiary, i.e. a frame stuffed with moss and a single plant grown in it.

Lyre topiary produced from Hedera helix 'Perfection'. This is a type 3 topiary, i.e. a single potted plant grown over a frame.

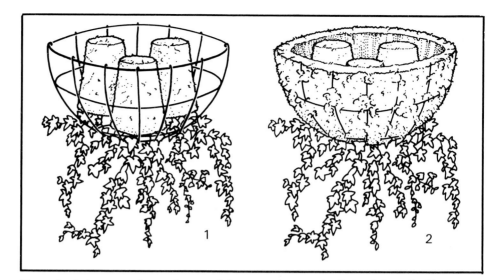

Practical instructions for making an ivy spiral and ivy ball

The previous examples show many very sophisticated pre-formed topiary structures requiring considerable expertise to produce them. Here and on page 137 two simple examples will be detailed so that the beginner can enjoy the decorative quality of this art form for himself or herself and obtain satisfaction from the creation of such topiary. At the end of the chapter there is a list of plants used in both America and Britain for this work, and maintenance instructions explain how to keep the topiary in good condition.

The examples which follow have deliberately been kept simple so as to make the first steps easy for a beginner. In America, simple frame shapes are readily available, as shown on pages 122 and 132, but this is not yet the case in Britain. The reader wishing to produce his or her own frame should refer to Chapter 4, where instructions on the making of frames are detailed. These instructions include details of the wire gauges needed (page 68).

To make an ivy ball

An excellent ivy for this purpose is 'Manda's Crested'.

1. Obtain two wire hanging baskets.
2. Take at least six plants of the same variety, with long hanging vines.

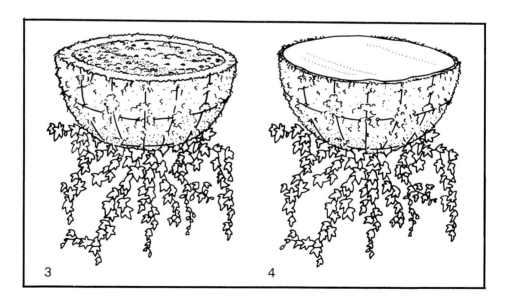

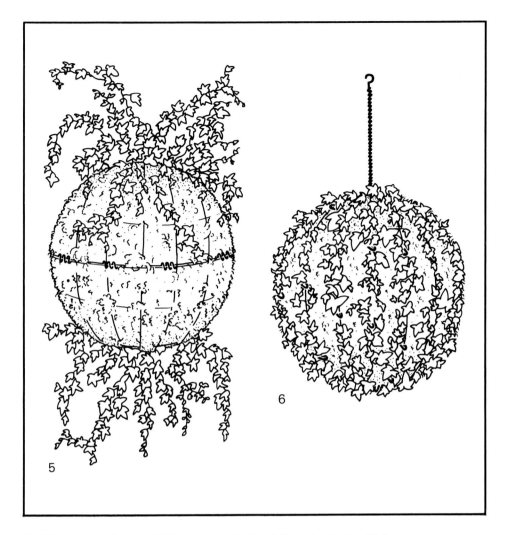

5

6

3. The more plants which are used, the fuller the ball will be.

4. Put three plants upside down in one basket so that the leaves of the vines hang through the wire at the bottom of the basket (Figure 1, opposite).

5. Line the basket with completely moist sphagnum moss and fill the hollow with good moist potting soil, putting it round the roots of the plants and up to the rim of the basket (Figures 2 and 3, opposite).

6. Do exactly the same with the other basket.

7. Place a large brown paper bag on top of one of the baskets — this will prevent the soil from spilling out when you turn the basket over, so that the two basket rims are together (Figures 4 and 5).

8. Pull the bag out from between the two rims once they are placed together.

9. Fasten both rims with wire to hold them together.

10. Anchor the ivy vines with hairpins to the ball, spreading out the vines evenly both up and down.

11. Hang the ball from the top by a long piece of wire with a hook at the end, attached to the centre of the ball (Figure 6, above).

Care of an ivy ball

1. Spray with fine mist every day.

2. Water entire topiary at least three times a week so that the moss is always moist.

3. Liquid feed leaves and roots once a month.

4. Clip ivy to keep the topiary round and neat.

Photo by Dick Keen, Longwood Gardens.

Photo by Dick Keen, Longwood Gar

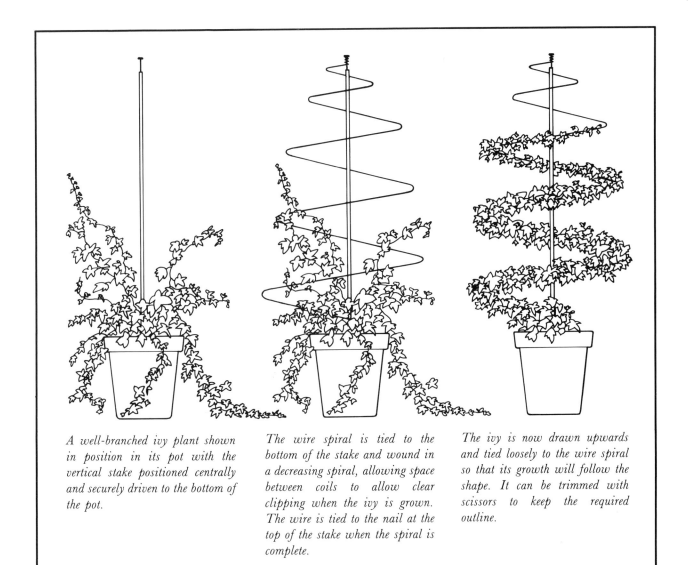

A well-branched ivy plant shown in position in its pot with the vertical stake positioned centrally and securely driven to the bottom of the pot.

The wire spiral is tied to the bottom of the stake and wound in a decreasing spiral, allowing space between coils to allow clear clipping when the ivy is grown. The wire is tied to the nail at the top of the stake when the spiral is complete.

The ivy is now drawn upwards and tied loosely to the wire spiral so that its growth will follow the shape. It can be trimmed with scissors to keep the required outline.

To make an ivy spiral

1. Get a strong stake.
2. Cut the stake to the length you want for the finished topiary.
3. Hammer a nail into the top of the stake to use as an anchor for the wire. Pot the chosen ivy plant as shown in the first drawing above.
4. Drive the stake firmly into the soil right to the centre of the bottom of the pot or container (see above).
5. Tie the wire to the bottom of the stake and shape the spiral, going from the widest dimension at the bottom and leaving enough space between spirals or coils so that the ivy will be cleanly clipped when grown up. When you reach the top of the spiral, fix the end of the wire to the nail at the top of the stake, as in the centre drawing above.
6. Tie the ivy branches loosely to the wire shape, trimming with scissors as necessary.

Opposite, top left, a pre-formed topiary dromedary standing majestically in Longwood's great hall; on the right, the front and back views of a lion at Longwood Gardens. The plant pots are to hold the hanging chrysanthemums which will form the lion's cloak. Ficus pumila (creeping fig) and Chlorophytum comosum (spider plant) are plants used for the lion's body. In the centre a circle of ivy at Meadowbrook; at the bottom a giraffe at Longwood Gardens.

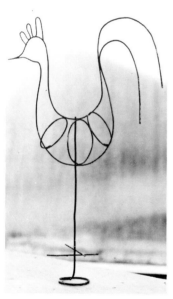

More of the frames which can be bought at garden centres and nurseries in the U.S.A.

Plants for pre-formed topiary

The most successful variety of plant used for this type of topiary is ivy of all descriptions but small-leaved varieties of other plants such as *Ficus pumila*, or creeping fig, and *Chlorophytum comosum* 'Vittatum' — the spider plant — are suitable for small frames. The plants used at Longwood Gardens in the U.S.A. are as follows:

Acorus gramineus 'Variegatus' — Japanese sweet-flag
Chlorophytum comosum 'Vittatum' — spider plant
Chrysanthemum x morifolium — cascading cultivars
Ficus pumila — creeping fig
Fittonia verschaffeltii var. argyroneura 'Minima' — silver-nerve fittonia
Guzmania 'Omer Moroboe' — bromeliad

Hedera helix

'Anne Marie'	'Gold Dust'	'Misty'
'Appaloosa'	'Green Feather'	'Nice Guy'
'Asterisk'	'Helena'	'Perfection'
'Boskoop'	'Hibernica'	'Pin Oak'
'Brokamp'	'Ingobert'	'Pirouette'
'Calico'	'Irish Lace'	'Pixie'
'California'	'Ivalace'	'Plume d'Or'
'California Gold'	'Jubilee'	'Serenade'
'Chicago'	'Kolbold'	'Shamrock'
'Dealbata'	'Kolibri'	'Shannon'
'Duck Foot'	'Leo Swicegood'	'Spetchley'
'Eva'	'Little Diamond'	'Telecurl'
'Fluffy Ruffle'	'Manda's Crested'	'Wichtel'
'Garland'	'Marie-Louise'	'Zebra'
'Gavotte'	'Merion Beauty'	
'Gertrud Strauss'	'Midget'	

Hedera nepalensis — 'Marbled Dragon'
Hedera rhombea — 'Variegata'
Myrtus sp. — myrtle
Pellionia daveauana
Pilea cadierei 'Minima' — dwarf aluminium plant
Pilea forgettii — paniminga or friendship plant
Pilea nummulariifolia — creeping Charley

Polystichium tsus-simense — table fern
Sagina subulata 'Aurea' — golden sagina
Selaginella kraussiana — trailing spike moss
Sempervivum spp.
Soleirolia soleirolii — baby's tears
Thymus pseudo-lanuginosus — woolly thyme

Dried materials
Glycerine leaves
Waxed flowers and leaves
(*Spathiphyllum*, *Anthurium* and *Palm*)

Steps leading up to two swans of ivy on frames at Meadowbrook.

General cultural instructions for maintaining completed pre-formed topiary kept indoors

1. Position — the ideal is a well-lit north window in summer but never in direct sunlight. In winter, a south position with little direct sunlight is ideal, but the moss should never be allowed to dry out completely.
2. Temperature should be between 55° and 70°F in winter.
3. Draughts, whether hot or cold, should be avoided.
4. Circulation of fresh air will assist in keeping the plant healthy and there should be some humidity in the room.
5. Watering should only be carried out to keep the soil evenly moist.
6. Dead or unwanted material should be cut off with scissors.
7. The plant will benefit from a shower of water at room temperature approximately once a month — place the pot in a plastic bag and tie it round the stem when showering, so as to avoid the spillage or soaking the soil.
8. The topiary should be turned once a week at least so as to get even growth.
9. Figures formed by stuffing moss into a frame should be shaped and misted over daily for the first two weeks. After that the normal schedule can be followed.
10. Areas such as tails, beak and all narrow sections will dry out first, so these should be given special attention.
11. Liquid feed should be administered regularly according to the manufacturer's instructions. It is generally used more frequently in the growing season.
12. With one-plant topiary it should not be forgotten that the root ball should be fed as well.
13. Ivies are suspectible to some diseases, red spider being the most frequent. A treatment should be administered, following the manufacturer's instructions carefully.
14. Pinning, pruning and grooming are vital on a regular basis. Keep the plant pinned close to the frame. Do not let the plant get too exuberant as this will cause the shape to distort.

Following these instructions will keep the topiary healthy and attractive, providing pleasure for a very long time.

Outside topiary of this type should also be turned and kept in a sheltered position. Regular watering is just as important and narrow sections should be given extra care to keep them moist. Peat-based compost is difficult to re-wet once dried.

Acknowledgements

First and foremost the author would like to thank her husband John Andrews, without whose help and support this book would not have been possible.

The author and publishers would also like to thank the following individuals, organisations and garden owners who have provided invaluable assistance in compiling this book.

United Kingdom

The National Trust
The National Gardens Scheme
Clive Crook
Brian Tomlin
Patrick Talbot-Smith
Clare Forte
Tony and Marion Morrison of South American Pictures
Sam Andrews
Lucy Boston
Capt. G.A. de G. Kitchin, C.B.E., R.N.
A.E. Powell
Kim and Rosie Kimber
Michael Boys
Rachel Crawshay, M.B.E.
Lizzie Graham of 'Travelling Secretaries', Uckfield
Great Dixter, Sussex
Chastleton Manor, Oxfordshire
Athelhampton, Dorset
Hever Castle, Kent
Sudeley Castle, Gloucestershire
Brickwall School, Northiam
Levens Heritage, Levens Hall, Cumbria
The Historic Gardens Trust, Sussex
Bill Mount of the Historic Gardens Trust
Mavis Batey, the Historic Garden Society
Frewen Educational Trust, Northiam
Buckinghamshire County Museum, curator Christopher Gowing, M.A., F.M.A.
Borough of Torbay, Parks and Recreation Services, Torquay, Devon
Mr. Carnell, designer of Torquay Exhibits at Chelsea Flower Show
Antique Collectors' Club, Suffolk
Lime Cross Nursery, Herstmonceux, Sussex
Royal Horticultural Society: Library — Vincent Square, London; Wisley
   Gardens, Surrey
Barry Ambrose, General Manager, R.H.S. Enterprises Ltd.

Discovering Topiary, by Margaret Baker, Shire Publications, 1969.
The Book of Topiary, by C. Curtis and W. Gibson, John Lane, 1904.
Garden Craftsmanship in Yew and Box, Nathaniel Lloyd, Ernest Benn, 1925.
Topiary and Ornamental Hedges, by Miles Hadfield, Adam & Charles Black.

Holland
Royal Netherlands Embassy
Al Elsholz
Jan Liewers
Ward van Klaveren

Italy
Villa Gamberaia, Settignano
Villa Garzoni, Collodi
Piccolomini Palace, Pienza

America
American Boxwood Society
The Boxwood Bulletin, Bluemont, Virginia
Mrs. Scot-Butler, co-editor of *The Boxwood Bulletin*

Mr. and Mrs. Liddon Pennock, Meadowbrook Farm, Pennsylvania
Charles O. Cresson, Horticulturalist, Meadowbrook Farm

John Enterline, Director of Conestoga House Foundation, Lancaster,
   Philadelphia

Longwood Gardens, Kennet Square, Pennsylvania
The staff of Longwood Gardens — especially:
Pat Hammer
Dick Keen
Mary Mizdail
Enola J.N. Teeter
Dave Thompson

Ladew Topiary Garden, Maryland

Eleanor Weller Jnr., Chairman of the Garden Club of America's Slide
   Library of Notable American Parks and Gardens

The American Ivy Society
Patricia Wellington-Jones, Editor of *The Ivy Journal,* American Ivy Society

Green Animals, Newport, Rhode Island

Mrs. Pannagio, Newport and Rhode Island Preservation Society

Mr. Robert Smith, Heronwood, Virginia

Mia Hardcastle, Topiary Inc., Tampa, Florida
Topiary Inc., Tampa, Florida, manufacturers of metal frames used at
   Longwood Gardens

June Mathews

Photographers

United Kingdom

Bob Bresset, *Westmorland Gazette*, 13

Britain on View Photographic Library (B.T.A.) (E.T.B.) of Levens Hall, 41, 73 (top)

Gamma Photography, Guildford, 60

Levens Hall Heritage, 13 (top), 103

Tony Morrison of South American Pictures, 78, 79

Borough of Torbay, Town Hall, Torquay, Devon, 128, 129

A. Vaughan Kimber, 22 (top), 32 (top), 65, 66, 88, 103 (top and centre left)

America

Dick Keen, Longwood Gardens, 115 (top and bottom left), 119, 124, 125, 133, 136 (top left and bottom)

Other photographs by Garden Art Press

Black and White Drawings

United Kingdom

David Crew, 20, 68, 69, 110, 111, 126, 227

Jack Hesketh, 64, 66, 97

Bill Mount, 85, 86, 87, 91, 92

Jane Porteous, 18, 34, 35, 36, 37, 38, 39, 42, 44, 47, 48, 49, 61, 62, 63, 134, 135, 137

America

Rachel Cobb, 130, 131, 132

Mia Hardcastle, Topiary Inc., Tampa, Florida, 122, 123 (drawings of carousel animals)

Mary Mizdail, Longwood Gardens, 122

Some Topiary Gardens Open to the Public

United Kingdom

The following are
National Trust gardens:
Antony, Cornwall
Ascott, Buckinghamshire
Barrington Court, Somerset
Blickling Hall, Norfolk
Canons Ashby, Northamptonshire
Castle Drogo, Devon
Chirk Castle, Clwyd
Hidcote Manor, Gloucestershire
Kingston Lacy, Dorset
Knightshayes, Devon
Lanhydrock, Cornwall
Little Moreton Hall, Cheshire
Lytes Cary, Somerset

Montacute, Somerset
Nymans, West Sussex
Packwood, Warwickshire
Peckover House, Cambridgeshire
Polesden Lacey, Surrey
Powis Castle, Powys
Saltram, Devon
Shugborough, Staffordshire
Sissinghurst Castle, Kent
Snowshill Manor, Gloucestershire
Tatton Park, Cheshire
Tintinhull, Somerset
Waddesdon Manor, Buckinghamshire
West Green House, Hampshire
Wightwick Manor, Staffordshire

Sudeley Castle, Gloucestershire.

The following are organisations which provide details of gardens open to the public at certain times of the year:

Gardens of England and Wales open to the public under the National Gardens Scheme, organised by the Queen's Institute of District Nursing. The Organising Secretary, The National Gardens Scheme, 57 Lower Belgrave Street, London, S.W.1.

Gardens open to the public, in aid of the Gardeners' Royal Benevolent Society and the Royal Gardeners' Orphan Fund. Bridge House, 139 Kingston Road, Leatherhead, Surrey KT22 7NT.

The Scottish National Trust, 12 Sherwood Street, London W1V 7RD.

Canons Ashby, Northamptonshire.

The National Trust. The Secretary, 36 Queen Anne's Gate, London, S.W.1.

Historic Houses, Castles and Gardens in Great Britain and Northern Ireland. Published annually by British Leisure Publications, Windsor Court, East Grinstead House, East Grinstead, West Sussex RH19 1XA.

Ulster Gardens Scheme. The Regional Information Officer, National Trust, Rowallane Saintfield, County Down.

America

Green Animals, Portsmouth, Rhode Island.
Ladew Topiary, Monkton, Maryland
Longwood Gardens, Kenneth Square, Pennsylvania

Blickling Hall, Norfolk.

Index